Learn Hiragana

STUDY GUIDE & WRITING PRACTICE

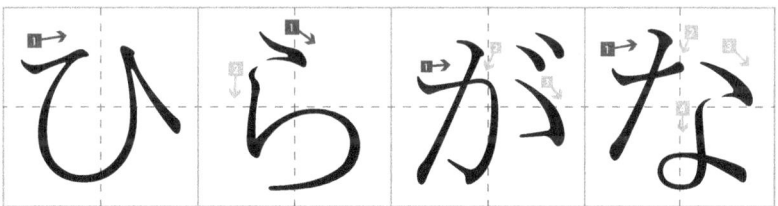

© Copyright 2020 George Tanaka
All Rights Reserved

POLYSCHOLAR

www.polyscholar.com

© **Copyright 2020 George Tanaka**
All Rights Reserved

Legal Notice: This book is copyright protected. This book is only for personal use. The content contained within this book may not be reproduced, duplicated or transmitted without direct written permission from the author or the publisher. You cannot amend, distribute, sell, use, quote or paraphrase any part of the content within this book, without the consent of the author or publisher.

CONTENTS

PART 1 Introduction 4
How to Use This Book 4
Background Information 5
Hiragana Chart 7
Modifiers & Rules 8
Writing Tips 10

PART 2 Learn to Write Hiragana 13

PART 3 Genkouyoushi 106

PART 4 Flash Cards 122

Tip: *This book works best with gel pens, pencils, biros and similar media. Take care with markers and ink, as heavy or wet media may result in paper bleed or transfer through to the pages below. Here are some test boxes to check how suitable your pens will be:*

Introduction

LEARNING JAPANESE

The first step in learning to read, write and speak Japanese is **Hiragana!** There is no doubt that seeing so many different symbols and shapes will be daunting to begin with. This book has been designed to make it **easier** and **quicker** to get to grips with.

We will start by going over some basic background information to give you a better understanding of how the whole language system works. After a *brief* look at the different 'alphabets' *(yes, there is more than one!)* we'll jump straight into learning Hiragana!

HOW TO USE THIS BOOK

As with learning any language, repetition is one of the fastest ways to soak it up. The second part of this workbook contains lots of carefully-designed instruction pages to help you learn how to write each character, with space to practice your Japanese writing skills:

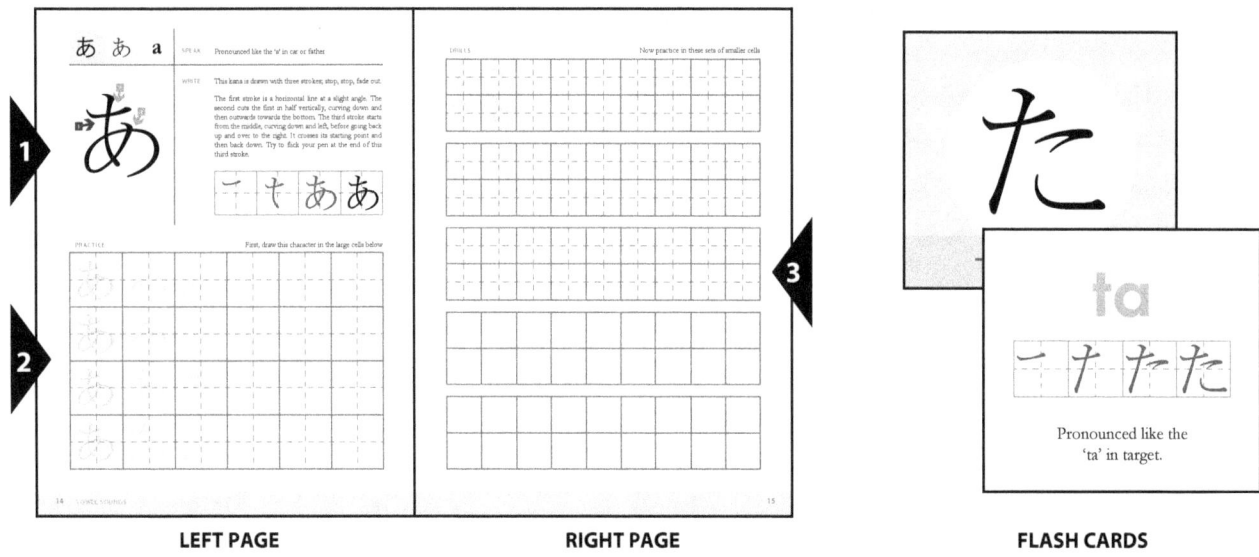

LEFT PAGE   **RIGHT PAGE**   **FLASH CARDS**

The third part of this workbook contains additional grids that you can use after you have learned how to write some *(or even all)* of the Hiragana. These pages are often referred to traditionally as *Genkouyoushi (or* 原稿用紙 *in Japanese)* which means 'manuscript paper'.

The final part of this workbook contains a set of flash card style pages that can either be photocopied or cut out. They are a great way to help you memorize the symbols and test your knowledge. *Younger learners should seek help from an adult to cut them out!*

JAPANESE SCRIPTS

Background

As you learn Japanese, you will encounter four very different types of scripts *(or alphabets)*. While this might sound complicated, this will start to make more sense in a moment - especially as you will already understand one of them!

RŌMAJI ロマジ

Literally meaning 'roman letters', this is really just a representation of the Japanese language using familiar English letters. It is only used to translate the language into a form that non-Japanese speakers can understand. It is not that common in every day use.

The other three scripts, **Hiragana**, **Katakana**, and **Kanji**, are used all the time and they are typically combined to make words and sentences in everyday Japanese writing. Each script has it's own purpose and together they tell us what word mean, where they come from, and also how we should say it.

HIRAGANA ひらがな

あいうえおかきくけこ

This is the first script we should learn and it consists of simple characters made with *round* shapes. Unlike the English alphabet, it is a **phonetic script** and each character represents a syllable sound. Each time you see a specific character, you will know how it sounds.

KATAKANA カタカナ

アイウエオカキクケコ

This is also a simple phonetic script. Katakana **represent the same syllable sounds as Hiragana** but are used for words *loaned* from other languages, such as foreign names, modern technology, or foods for example. Their appearance is more *angular and spikey*.

KANJI 漢字

Translated as 'Chinese letters', **Kanji** are characters borrowed from the Chinese language. Unlike the other scripts that represent sounds, **Kanji** symbols show blocks of meaning, like whole words, or a general idea about something.

年 本 月 生 米 前 合 事 社 京

There are literally *thousands* of Kanji, and new ones are being created all the time, so they are quite a challenge for even the most advanced linguists. There is some logic to how they are made so *eventually* you can understand or guess symbols you haven't seen before.

A LOOK AT HIRAGANA

There are **46 basic Hiragana** characters that, unlike English letters, each represent a different spoken sound instead of a letter. Virtually all of these sounds are based on just 5 'vowels sounds' - when you see how it works, I promise it will seem a lot easier!

Hiragana	あ	い	う	え	お
Romaji	a	i	u	e	o
Pronunciation	'ah'	'ee'	'oo'	'eh'	'oh'

The Five Vowel Sounds

This book will show you how to write all the basic Hiragana and also how extra sounds can be created by combining the basic symbols. By the end of the book, you will be able to write the characters that make up most of the sounds you will need for Japanese.

The next few pages contain a lot of information but try not to let this overwhelm you. In addition to the chart of basic Hiragana that you will learn, we will break down some of the basic rules to combining these symbols. And then, we'll put pen to paper!

Hiragana Chart

This chart shows the 46 basic Hiragana with a *spelling* in Romaji for a similar phonetic sound. The vowel sounds are at the top and their counterpart versions with consonant sounds are shown below them. **note the exception 'n' - also, *wo is an uncommon kana.*

Vowel Sounds

	a	i	u	e	o
	あ a	い i	う u	え e	お o
k	か ka	き ki	く ku	け ke	こ ko
s	さ sa	し shi	す su	せ se	そ so
t	た ta	ち chi	つ tsu	て te	と to
n	な na	に ni	ぬ nu	ね ne	の no
h	は ha	ひ hi	ふ fu	へ he	ほ ho
m	ま ma	み mi	む mu	め me	も mo
y	や ya		ゆ yu		よ yo
r	ら ra	り ri	る ru	れ re	ろ ro
w	わ wa		ん **n		を *wo

Consonants

Basic Hiragana Chart

Modifiers

DIACRITICS

In addition to the *basic Hiragana*, there are 25 **Diacritic** symbols. They are used for similar sounding syllables that are voiced differently. They are essentially the same basic symbols but with extra marks to show they should be pronounced with a slightly altered sound:

| Basic | with Dakuten | with Handakuten |

Basic Hiragana with these small strokes *(Dakuten)* or a circle *(Handakuten)* above them show that the consonant part of the sound needs to be changed when spoken:

- **k**-sound are pronounced with a **g**-sound.
- **s**-sounds change to a **z**-sound *(except for し)*.
- **t**-sounds become **d**-sounds.
- **h**-sounds become **b**-sounds with *Dakuten*.
  ...or **P**-sounds with the *Handakuten*.

	a	i	u	e	o
k ▶ g	が ga	ぎ gi	ぐ gu	げ ge	ご go
s ▶ z	ざ za	じ ji	ず zu	ぜ ze	ぞ zo
t ▶ d	だ da	ぢ dzi (ji)	づ dzu	で de	ど do
h ▶ b	ば ba	び bi	ぶ bu	べ be	ぼ bo
h ▶ p	ぱ pa	ぴ pi	ぷ pu	ぺ pe	ぽ po

8 Modifiers

DIGRAPHS

This set of symbols are called **Digraphs** - using two basic characters we have already seen, they show where two syllable sounds are combined to create a new one:

き + や = きゃ
(ki) (ya) (kya)

When writing these letters, it is vital that the second symbol is drawn noticeably smaller than the first. This is how we can tell that the two sounds should be combined.

Pronunciation of these so-called *compound Hiragana* sounds is quite simple - for example, き (ki) + や (ya) becomes きゃ (kya) and we pronounce it like 'kiya' *without the 'i' sound.*

Don't let the chart below scare you - all of the Digraphs are made *exclusively* with letters from the い/i column *(excluding itself)* **and** they are only modified by letters from row **Y**!

きゃ kya	きゅ kyu	きょ kyo	ぎゃ gya	ぎゅ gyu	ぎょ gyo
しゃ sha	しゅ shu	しょ sho	じゃ ja	じゅ ju	じょ jo
ちゃ cha	ちゅ chu	ちょ cho	にゃ nya	にゅ nyu	にょ nyo
ひゃ hya	ひゅ hyu	ひょ hyo	びゃ bya	びゅ byu	びょ byo
ぴゃ pya	ぴゅ pyu	ぴょ pyo	りゃ rya	りゅ ryu	りょ ryo
みゃ mya	みゅ myu	みょ myo			

Modifiers

Modifiers

DOUBLE CONSONANTS

We also need to be aware that some Japanese words contain a *double consonant sound*. When written, these words contain an extra symbol in the form of a small つ/**tsu** *(called sokuon)* to show that it needs to be pronounced differently. Let's look at an example:

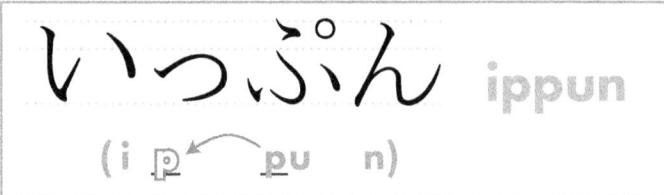

Without the small つ *(tsu)*, the word いぷん *(ipun)* doesn't have any meaning but いっぷん *(ippun)*, with the *sokuon*, means (a) minute.

Notice that the small つ is placed **before** the character that it takes the extra consonant sound from. When you see words with this modifier, the consonant part of the symbol that follows it *(in this example, the 'p' from 'pu')* is added to the end of the sound before it.

Both consonants need to be heard separately when the word is spoken, like saying **'ip-pun'** but without leaving a gap than can be heard.

LONG VOWEL SOUNDS

Just as there are double consonant sounds, we need to be aware of elongated vowel sounds too *(e.g. aa, ii. oo, ee, and uu)*. When speaking, we simply extend the duration of the sound (usually double) but in writing these words, the long vowel sound is shown with an additional character *(called a chouon)*. The character used varies depending on the vowel:

Vowel	Extender
a	あ
i / e	い
u / o	う

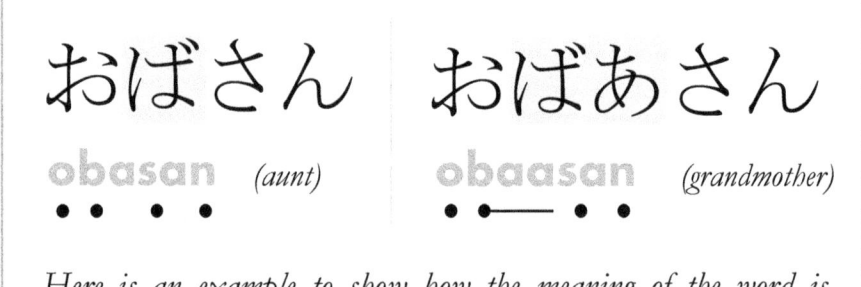

Here is an example to show how the meaning of the word is changed by adding (or missing) the longer vowel sound!

The Japanese language is full of exceptions but they tend to be learned with experience. It's just useful to be aware of double consonants and vowels for now, so you can understand when you see one!

Writing Tips

WRITING DIRECTION

Traditionally, Japanese text was arranged in vertical columns and written/read one column at a time from top to bottom and starting at the right side of the page. Since the end of the Second World War, the more familiar horizontal orientation is used - read left to right, just as in the English language. This applies to each of the different scripts.

The text in these examples is identical, except for the reading and writing direction:

1.
私は犬を飼っています。
彼女は行儀が良い。
彼らは寝るのが好きです。
多くの場合、一日中。
多分彼女は怠け者です。

2.
私は犬を飼っています。
彼女は行儀が良い。
彼らは寝るのが好きです。
多くの場合、一日中。
多分彼女は怠け者です。

Tategaki
縦書き
('vertical writing')

Yokogaki
横書き
('horizontal writing')

Both of these styles are accepted and are often chosen based on the layout and design of the document. Generally speaking, vertical layouts are used for traditional texts, while horizontal text is found in more modern, official documents or writing. One thing to remember is that books with the *tategaki* vertical writing style are bound the opposite way to English books, so you actually start reading them from the back cover to the front!

PRONUNCIATION

Learning to pronounce Japanese well begins with Hiragana as it covers a lot of the sounds we need for the whole language. It's important to practice at this early stage if you want to develop a natural and native sounding accent.

Note: This workbook includes a very basic introduction to Japanese pronunciation, as this is taught most effectively with audio. Each of the practice pages uses a similar sounding word or syllable from English to describe the sounds. It is good practice to repeat them out loud as you progress through the book.

Writing Tips

STROKES & LINES

Japanese scripts are traditionally written with a brush and have an inky, painted look. Even though we use modern pens now, it's important that we learn to write traditionally, with the same movements and **strokes**. Conveniently, Hiragana け *(or 'ke')* contains all three stroke types - we have named them based on how they are made and look:

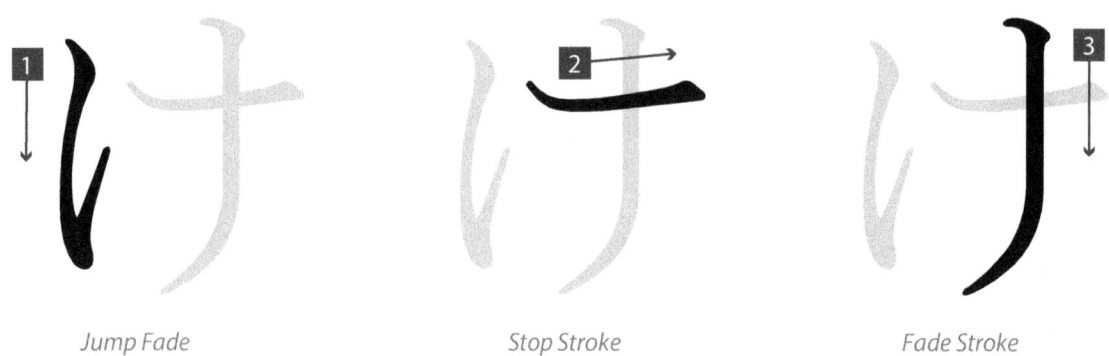

Jump Fade   *Stop Stroke*   *Fade Stroke*

The "**jump fade**" is made with a quick flick of the pen from the paper at the end of that stroke. The "**stop stroke**" is exactly how it sounds, where you bring the line to a definite stop before lifting your pen. The "**fade stroke**" is made by lifting your pen more gently from the paper while your hand is still in motion. You can imagine how the line might get thinner and fade out if you were gradually lifting a thicker brush tip from the page.

WRITING STYLES

This book will teach you how to write Hiragana with the standard movements based on brushed appearances, but you will encounter other styles as you learn:

These characters all have the same meaning but look a little different because they are made either by hand, with pens or pencils, or displayed as a modern digital font on a screen or in print. Even though the appearance changes slightly, the meaning remains.

Part 2

LEARN HOW TO WRITE HIRAGANA

あ　あ　a

SPEAK　Pronounced like the 'a' in car or father, but shorter.

LEARN　This kana is drawn with three strokes; stop, stop, fade out.

The first stroke is a horizontal line at a slight angle. The second cuts the first in half vertically, curving down and then outwards towards the bottom. The third stroke starts from the middle, curving down and left, before going back up and over to the right. It crosses its starting point and then back down. Try to flick your pen at the end of this third stroke.

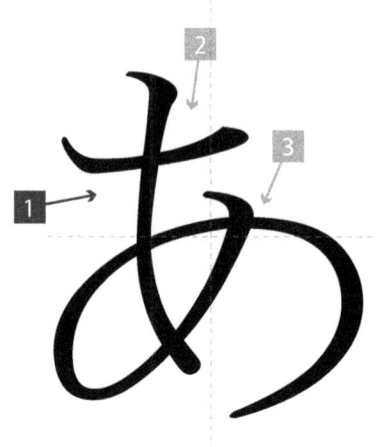

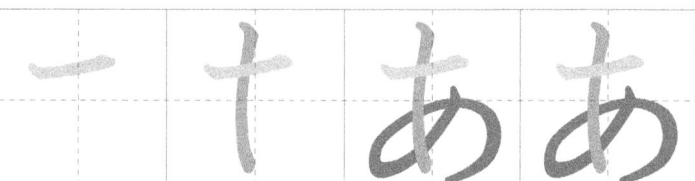

WRITE　　　　　　　　　　　　First, draw this character in the large cells below

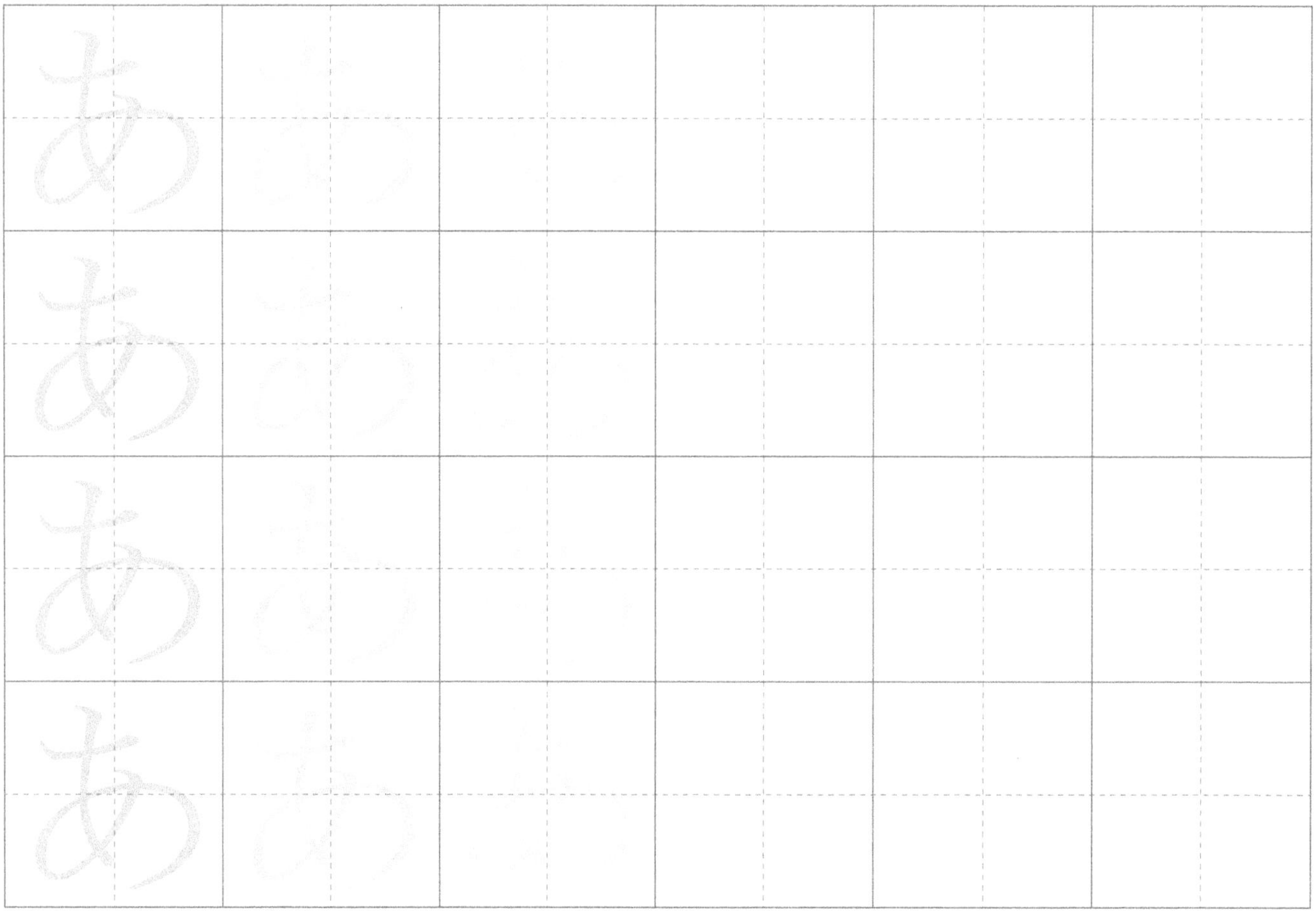

PRACTICE   Now practice in these sets of smaller cells

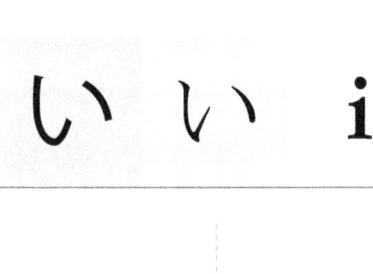

SPEAK — Pronounced like the 'ee' in eel.

LEARN — This kana is drawn with two strokes; jump fade, stop.

The first stroke is a curved diagonal line that turns sharply upwards at the bottom, ending with a pen flick. This kind of release with a sharp turn is called a hane. When writing a hane, it is as though this stroke is connecting to the next. The second stroke starts almost where your first stops - draw an opposite curving line from the first stroke, shorter than the first, without the hane.

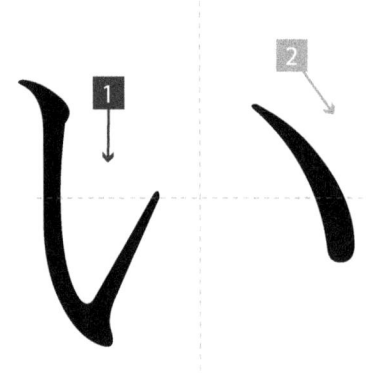

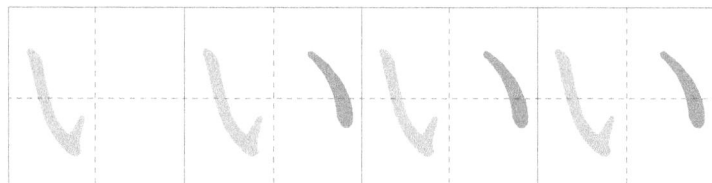

WRITE — First, draw this character in the large cells below

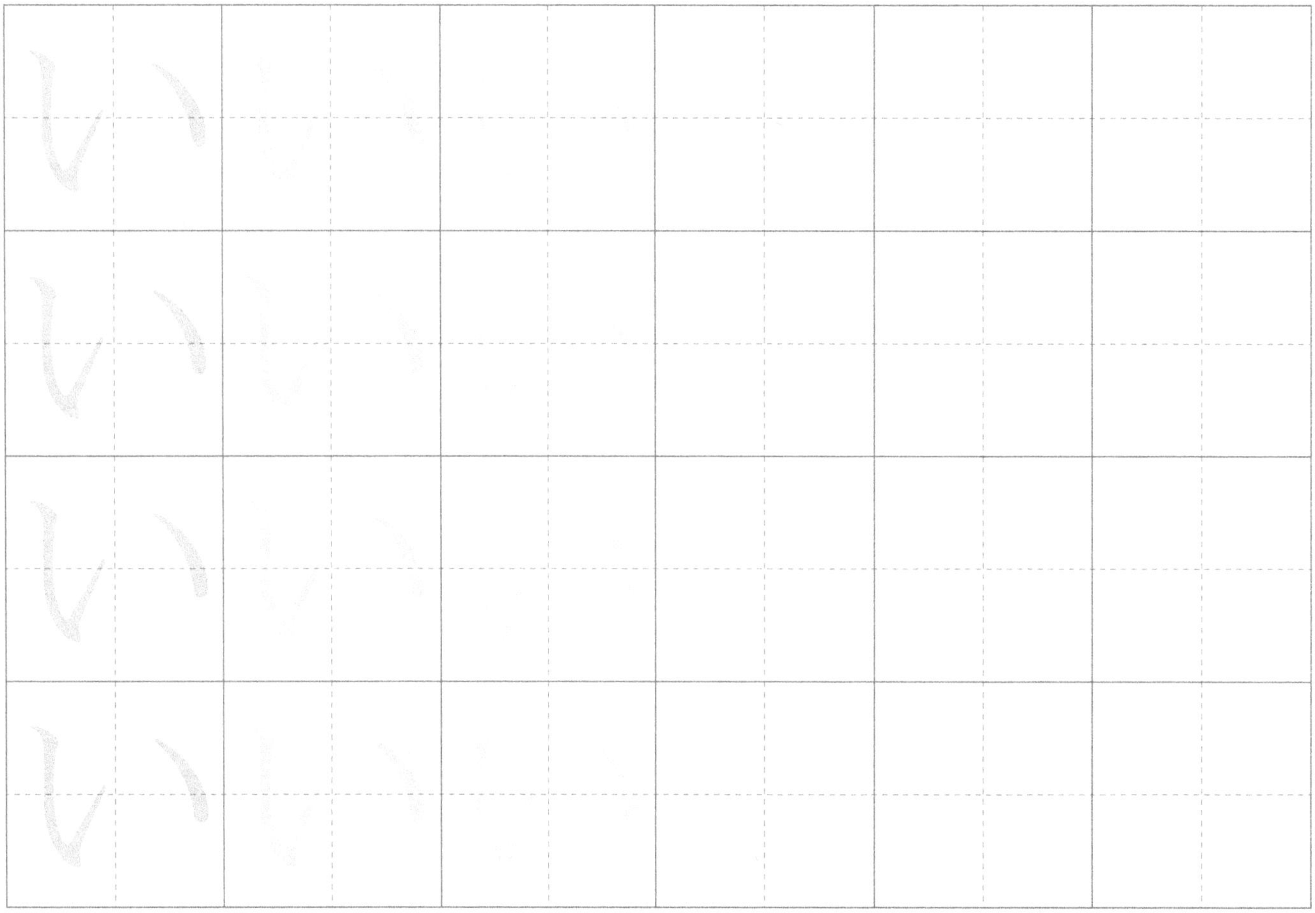

PRACTICE   Now practice in these sets of smaller cells

う う **u**

SPEAK　Pronounced like the 'oo' in zoo.

LEARN　This kana is drawn with two strokes; jump fade, stop.

Draw the short slanted line at the top center, and flick your pen back and away to the left. Be mindful of the second stroke as you flick the pen away - it begins almost where the first ended, in the same direction. The ear shape curves up to the right and then down to the bottom center. Flick your pen as you complete this stroke too. The first stroke doesn't want to be too big or it will look off balance.

WRITE　First, draw this character in the large cells below

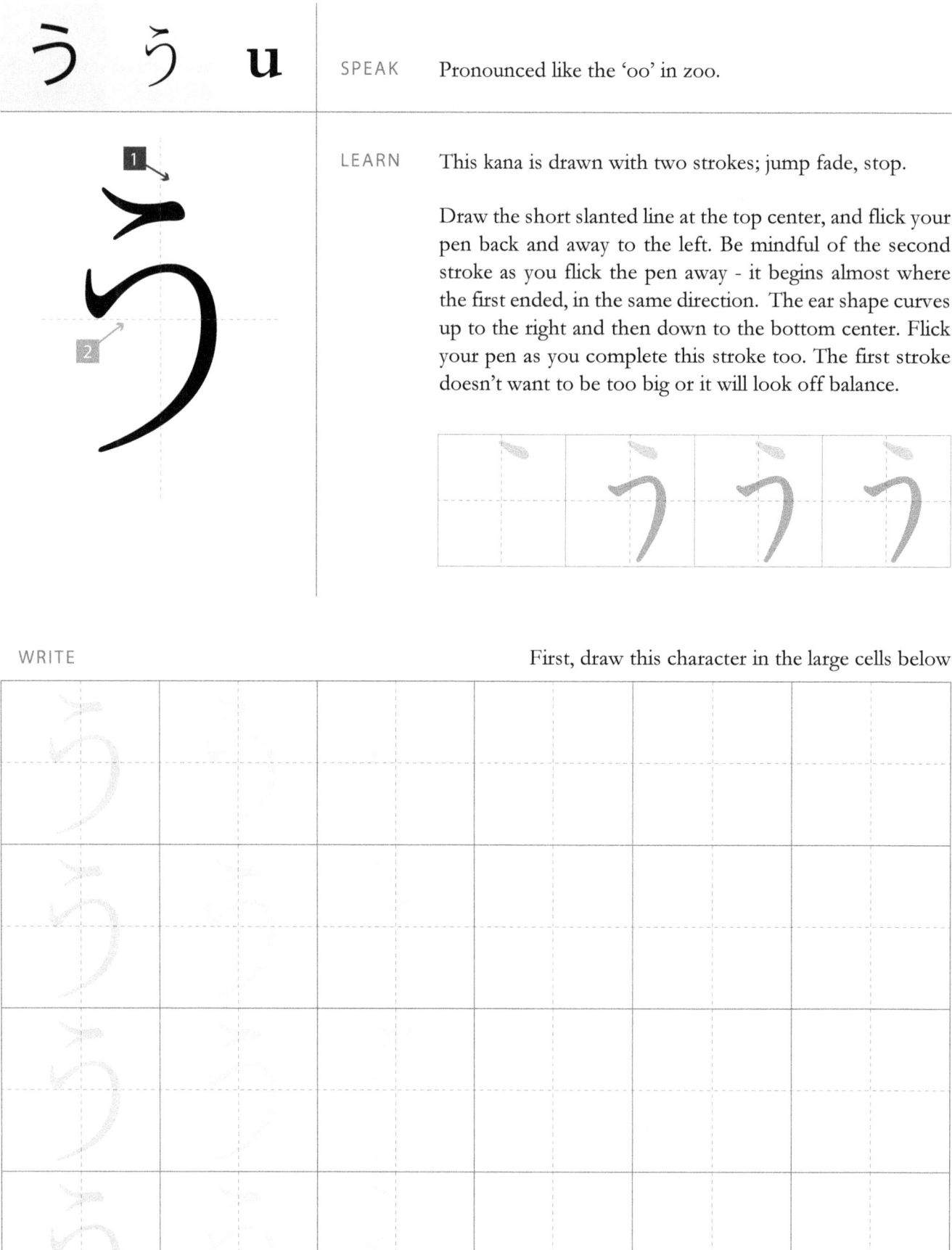

PRACTICE Now practice in these sets of smaller cells

え え **e**

SPEAK   Pronounced as 'eh' like the 'e' in men.

LEARN   This kana is drawn with two strokes; jump fade, stop.

We start just like the previous hiragana う, with a short slanted line at the top in the center. For the second stroke, imagine writing the number 7 and then tracing up a little, before drawing a small wave. Extend this stroke but don't flick the pen off the page.

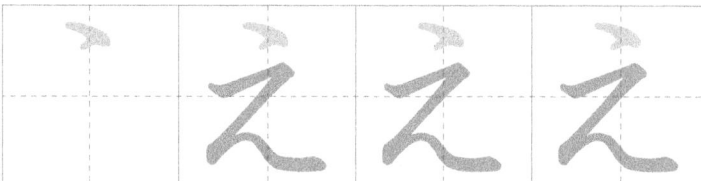

WRITE   First, draw this character in the large cells below

PRACTICE Now practice in these sets of smaller cells

お お o

SPEAK Pronounced like the 'o' in original.

LEARN This kana is drawn with three strokes; stop, fade, stop.

Start with a short horizontal line, just as with あ, but a little lower and to the left. The second stroke cuts the first in half with a vertical line, turning sharply to the left at the bottom. It then turns again to create a large curve before flicking your pen off at the end. The third small stroke positioned up to the top right of the first stroke.

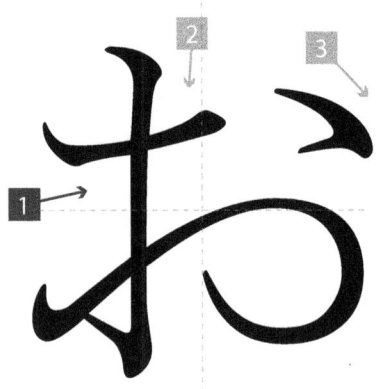

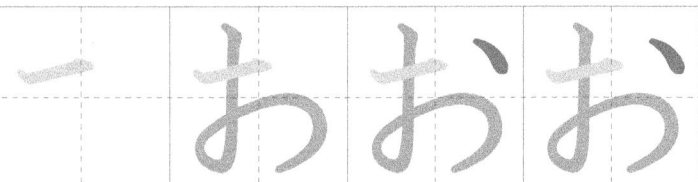

WRITE First, draw this character in the large cells below

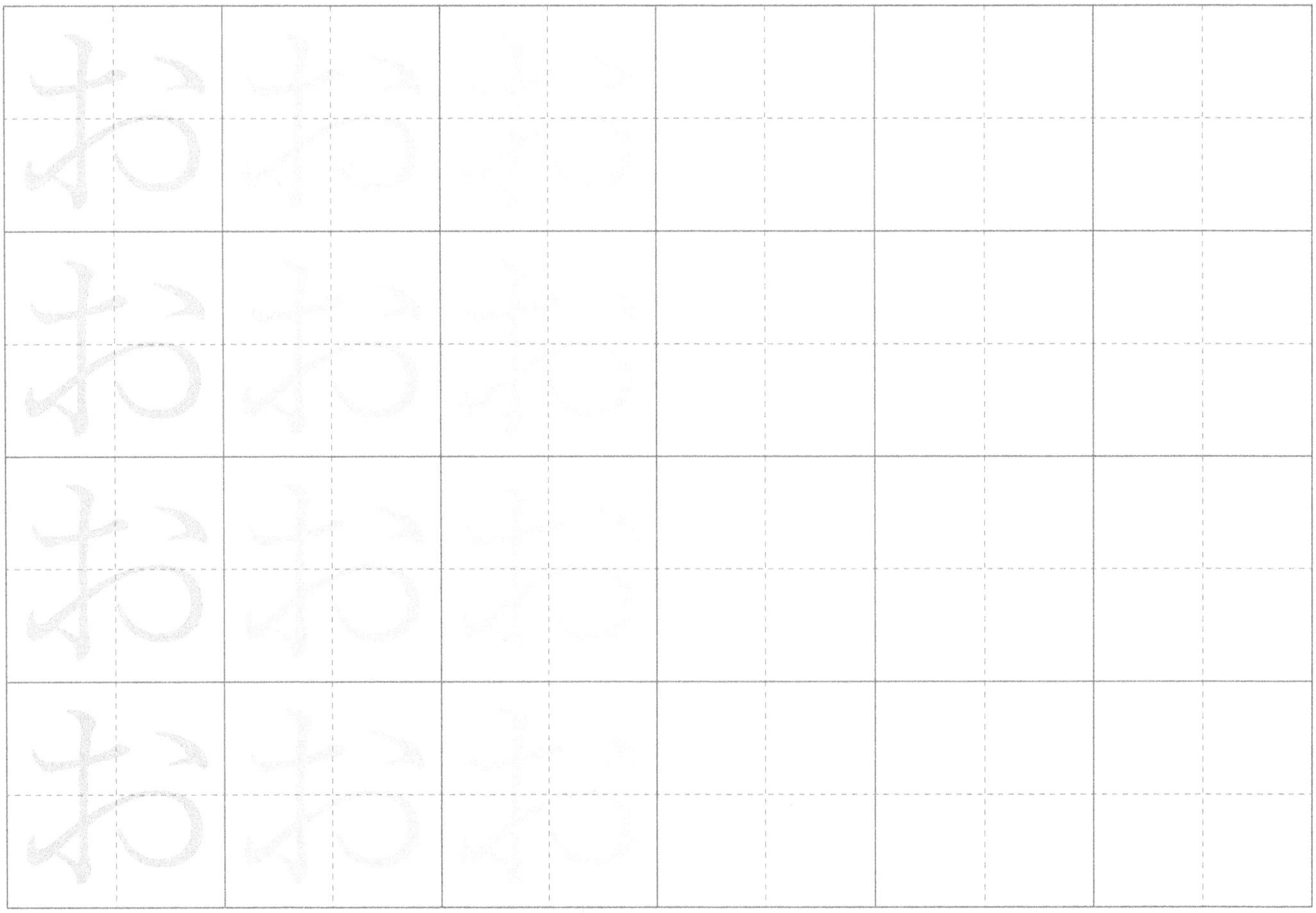

PRACTICE   Now practice in these sets of smaller cells

か　か　**ka**

SPEAK　Pronounced like 'car' but without the 'r' sound.

LEARN　This kana is drawn with three strokes; jump, stop, stop.

Start with a horizontal line before turning vertically down, and bending back to the left - end with a *hane*. The second stroke intersects the first, from upper middle to lower left. The final stroke is a slanted curve over to the right of. It is important that this stroke is longer than the small strokes in previous kana, to ensure it is not read as a modifier.

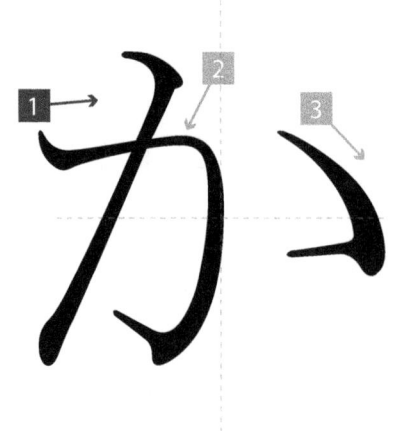

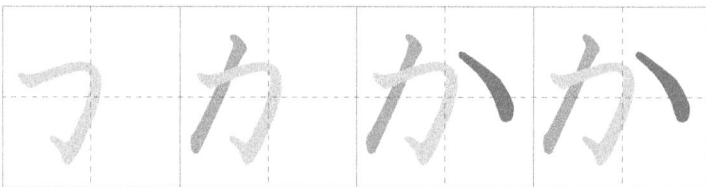

WRITE　First, draw this character in the large cells below

PRACTICE   Now practice in these sets of smaller cells

き き **ki**

SPEAK   Pronounced like 'key'.

LEARN   Drawn with four strokes; stop, stop, jump fade, stop.

Your first two strokes are parallel lines, from left to right, and at a slight angle. Stroke three cuts through the first two, and ends with a *hane*. Draw your hane moving upwards, setting up the fourth mark. Draw the last curved stop mark around to the right. You often see these marks connected in some fonts, as shown in the small image on the left, but this is the correct way to draw this character.

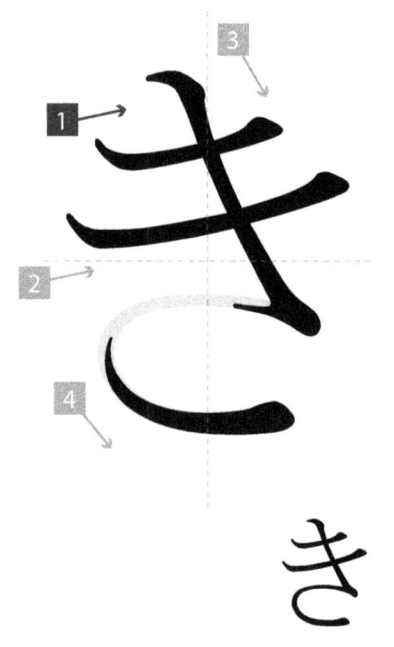

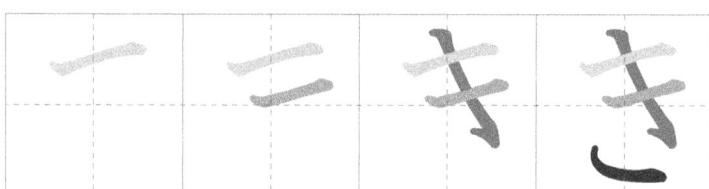

WRITE   First, draw this character in the large cells below

26

PRACTICE   Now practice in these sets of smaller cells

く く **ku**

SPEAK Pronounced like the 'koo' in cuckoo.

LEARN This kana is drawn with just one stroke: a stop.

This single stroke character is drawn much like an opening angle bracket, but with a slight bend inwards. Try to make sure that the start and end points are aligned vertically, to create a neat balanced character.

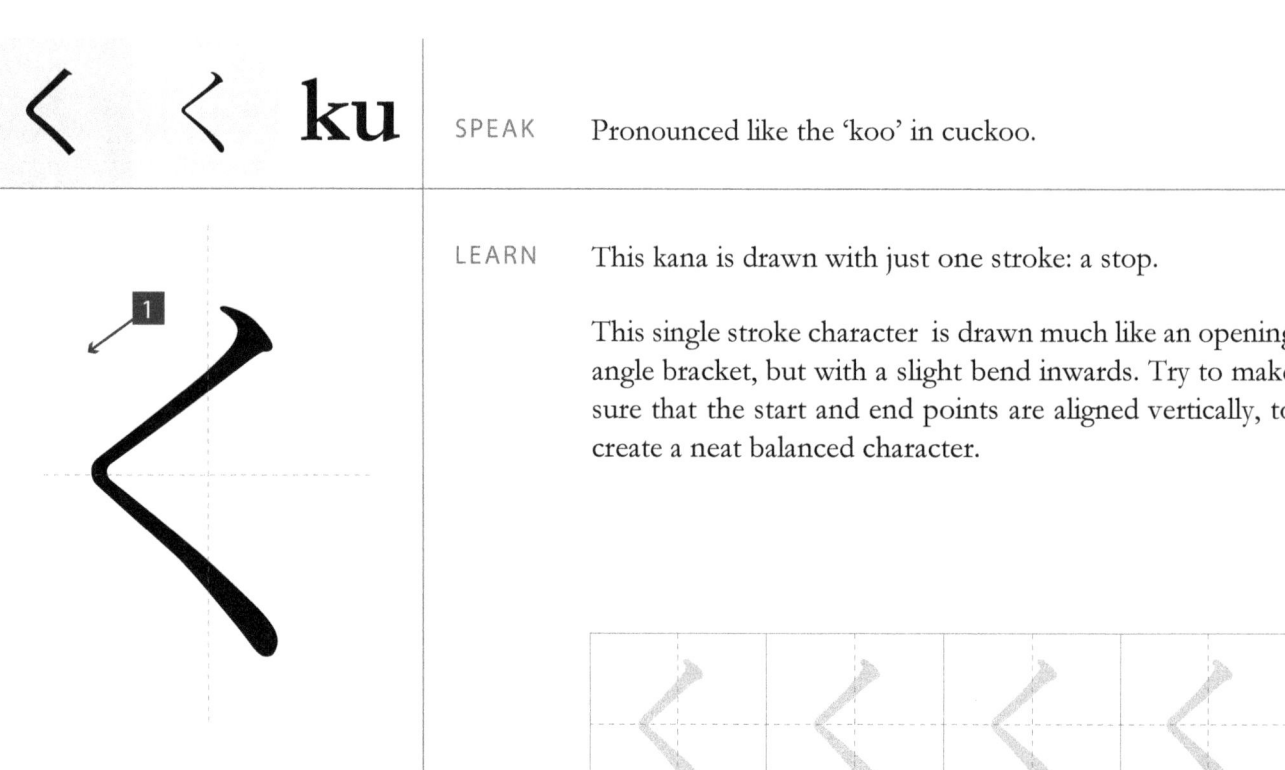

WRITE First, draw this character in the large cells below

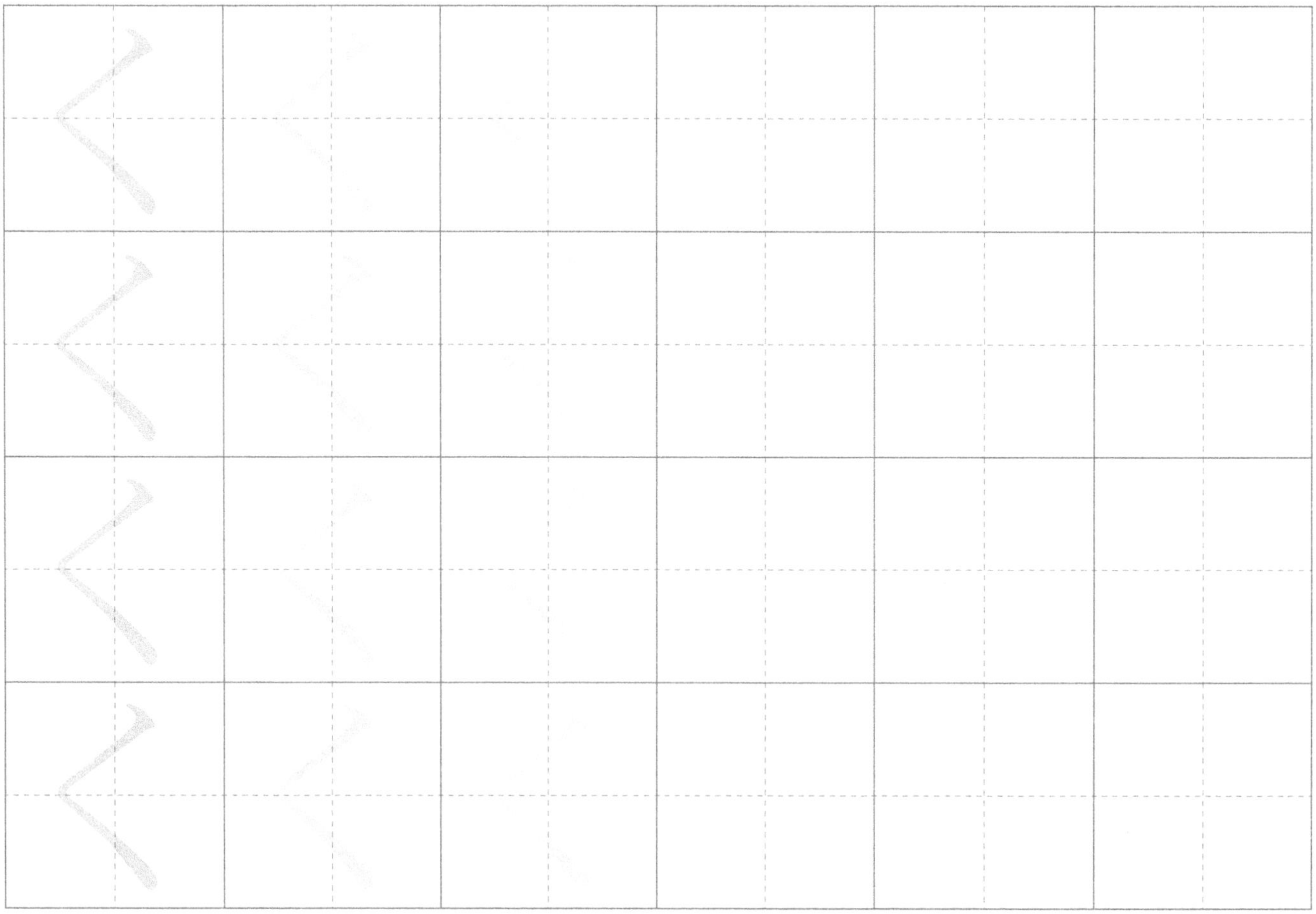

PRACTICE   Now practice in these sets of smaller cells

け け **ke**

SPEAK   Pronounced like the 'ke' in Kenneth

LEARN   This kana has three strokes: a jump fade, a stop, and a fade.

Draw the first stroke downwards with a bit of a curve outwards and ending with a hane. The second mark is made as a continuation from the hane, with a short line left to right. Your last stroke is another vertical line down, with a curve to the left this time. It starts a little higher than before, and ends lower too. Finish this stroke with a flick of your pen.

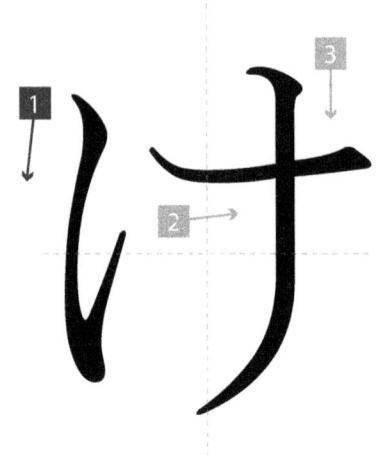

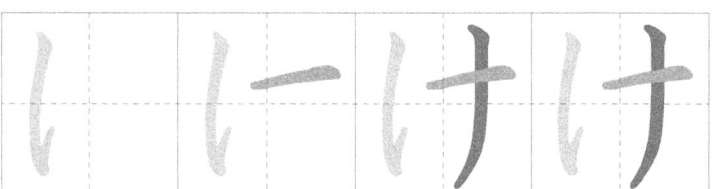

WRITE   First, draw this character in the large cells below

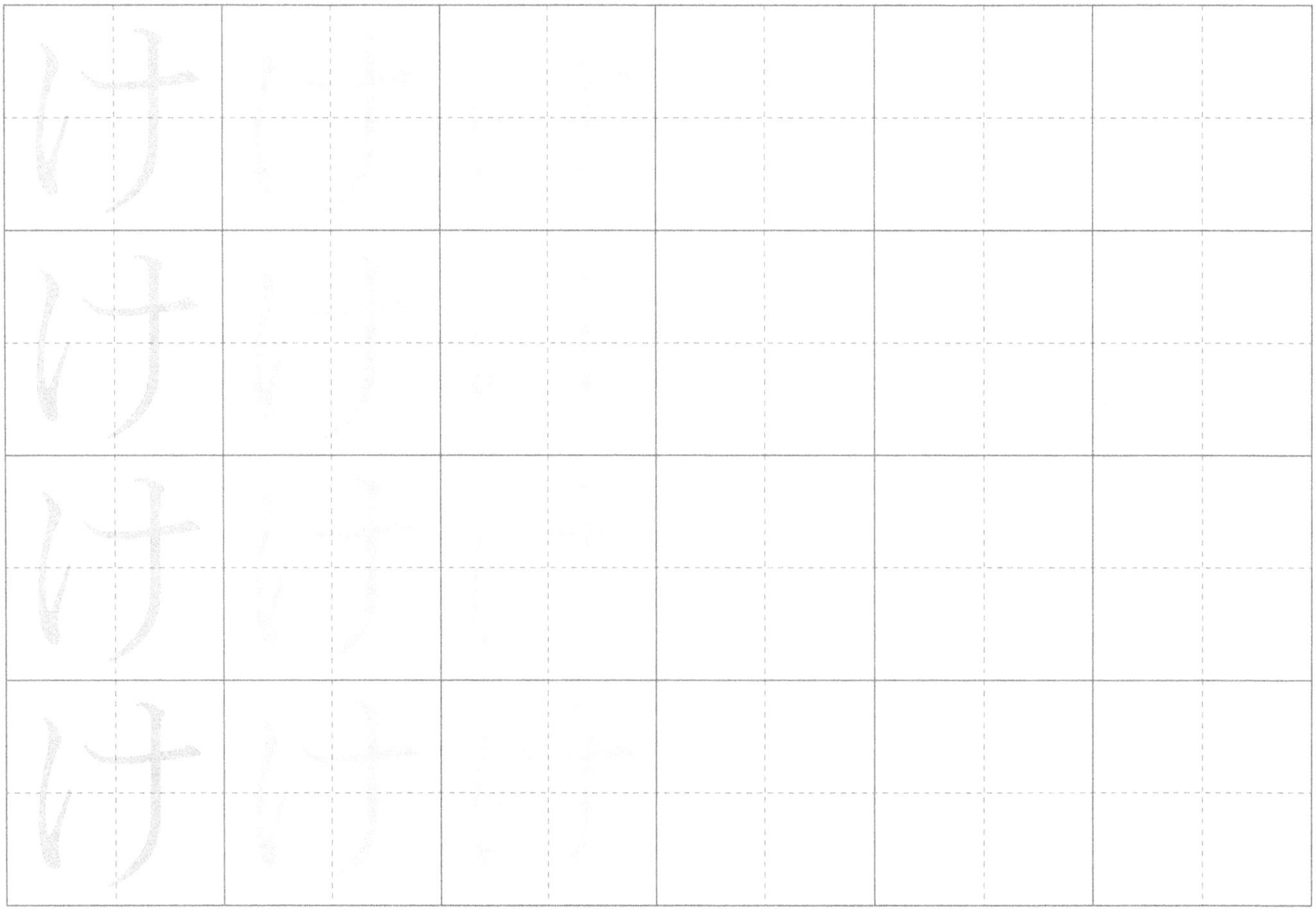

PRACTICE

Now practice in these sets of smaller cells

こ こ **ko**

SPEAK — Pronounced like the 'co' in core

LEARN — This kana is drawn with two strokes: a jump and a stop.

Draw this kana is with two strokes that curve inwards almost connecting to make a large loop. The first mark is a curved horizontal line ending with a hane. Your second stroke starts lower down and to the left. The strokes should look as though they are almost connecting to create a closed circular shape.

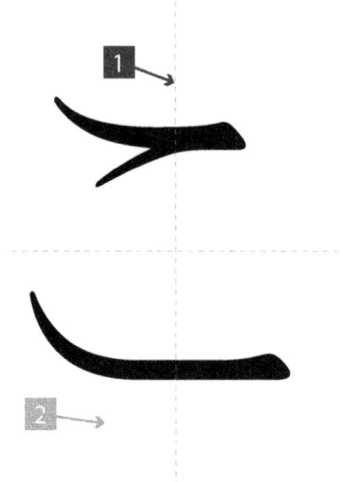

WRITE — First, draw this character in the large cells below

PRACTICE   Now practice in these sets of smaller cells

さ さ **sa**	
	SPEAK — Pronounced like the 'sa' in sardines.

LEARN — This kana is drawn with three strokes: stop, jump, stop

Written in a similar way to き but without the first short stroke. Start with the angled horizontal line from left to right. Your second stroke cuts through this mark and ends with a hane. The third mark is made by putting your pen down slightly after the hane and curving back around. This kana is often displayed as being connected but the correct method is to lift your pen.

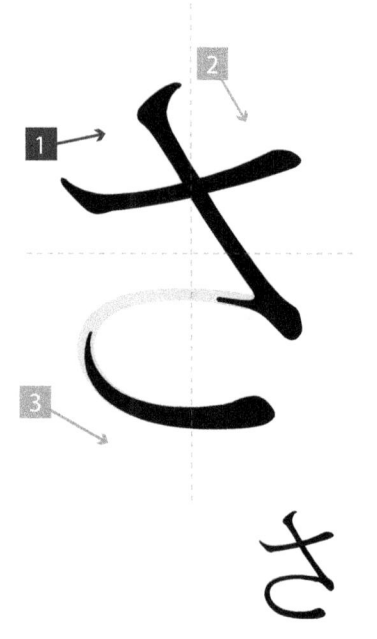

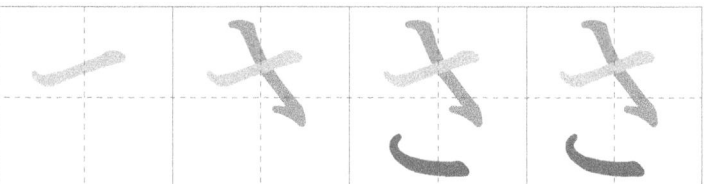

WRITE — First, draw this character in the large cells below

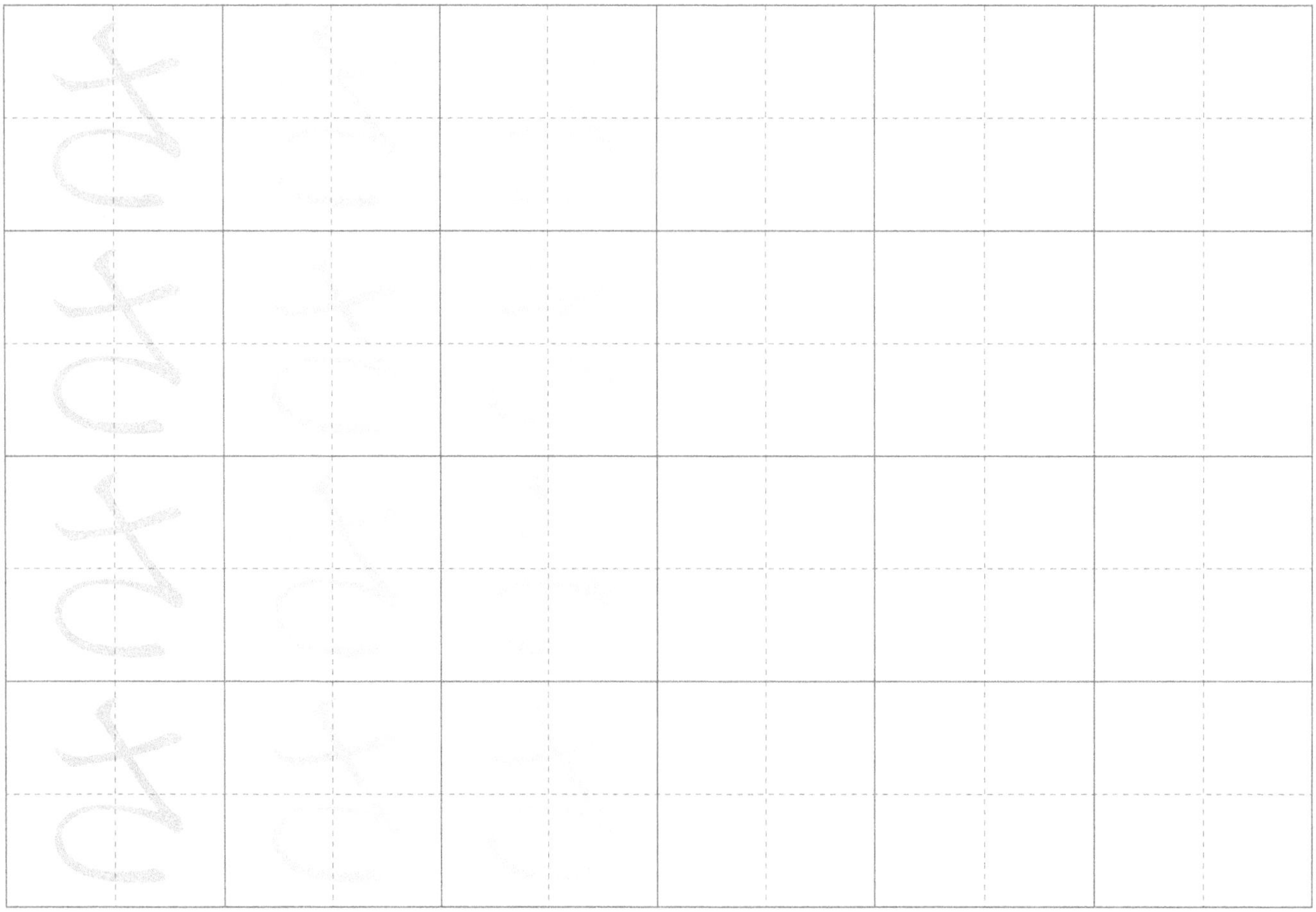

PRACTICE Now practice in these sets of smaller cells

し　し　shi

SPEAK — Pronounced like 'she' as in sheet.

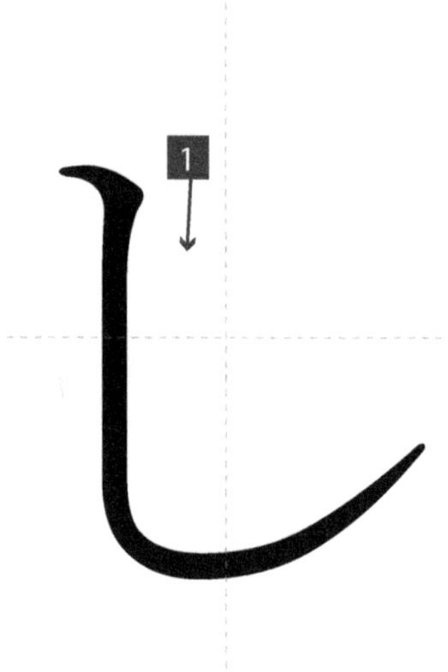

LEARN — Draw this kana with a single stroke; a brushed fade.

This kana is written with just one stroke. It begins as a vertical line from top to bottom before curving out to the right and upwards. Flick your pen from the page at the end.

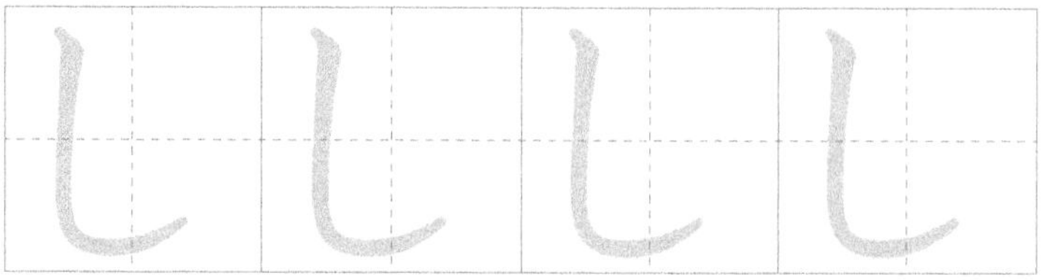

WRITE

First, draw this character in the large cells below

PRACTICE　　　　　　　　　　　　　　　　　　　Now practice in these sets of smaller cells

す　す　su

SPEAK — Pronounced like the 'su' in super

LEARN — This has two strokes; a stop, and a looping fade.

Begin with a long line drawn from left to right. Your second mark starts at the top and is drawn down through the first. It then creates a loop just after the intersection. Complete the stroke by curving down to the left and flick your pen from the paper at the end to fade the stroke out. Try to cut through the first stroke slightly off center, to the right. This will create more space for your loop below.

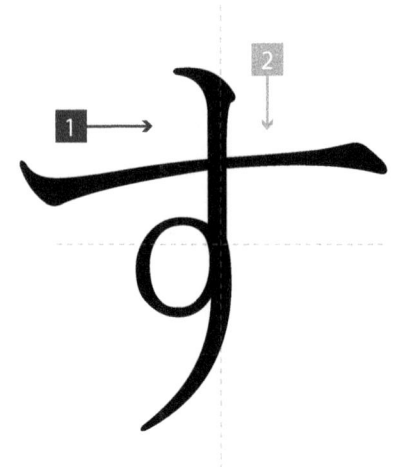

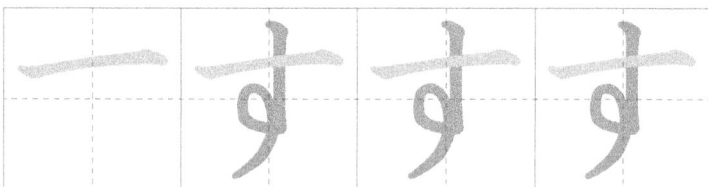

WRITE — First, draw this character in the large cells below

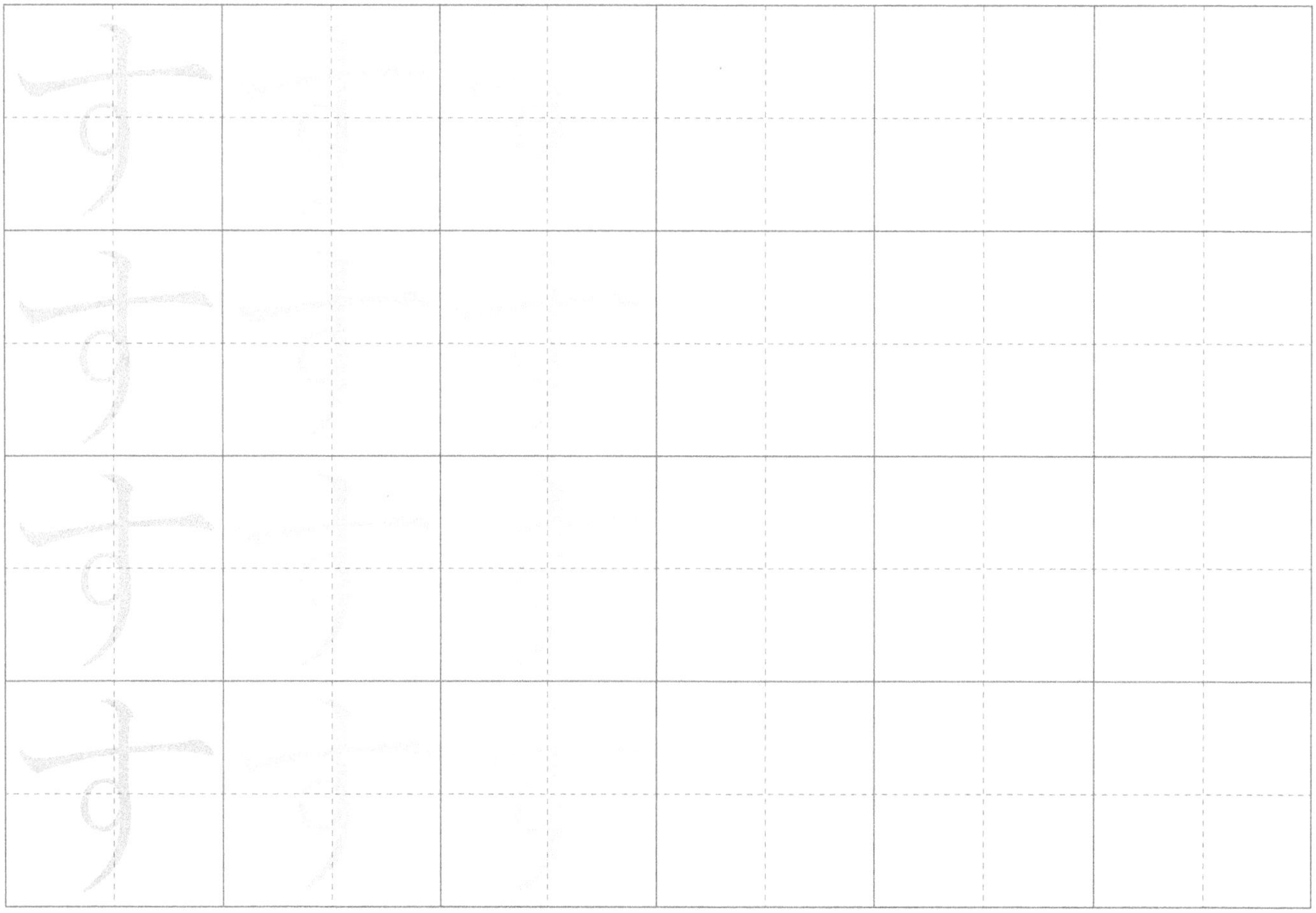

PRACTICE   Now practice in these sets of smaller cells

せ せ **se**

SPEAK   Pronounced like 'say' but with less 'y'.

LEARN   This kana is drawn with three strokes; stop, jump, stop

Begin this character with a long horizontal line, left to right. The second stroke is a shorter, vertical line to the right side and ends with a hane upwards and left. Lift your pen but keep momentum in the same direction as you set up for the third stroke. Make a vertical line down and bend around and to the right. Don't flick your pen here. The first two marks should cut through the first with even spaces.

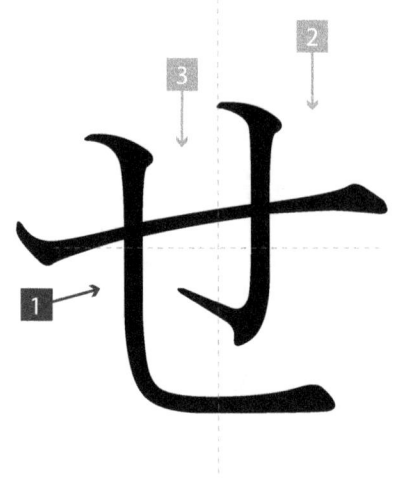

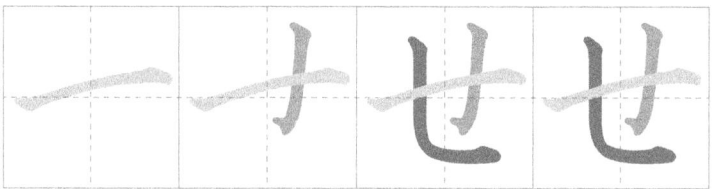

WRITE   First, draw this character in the large cells below

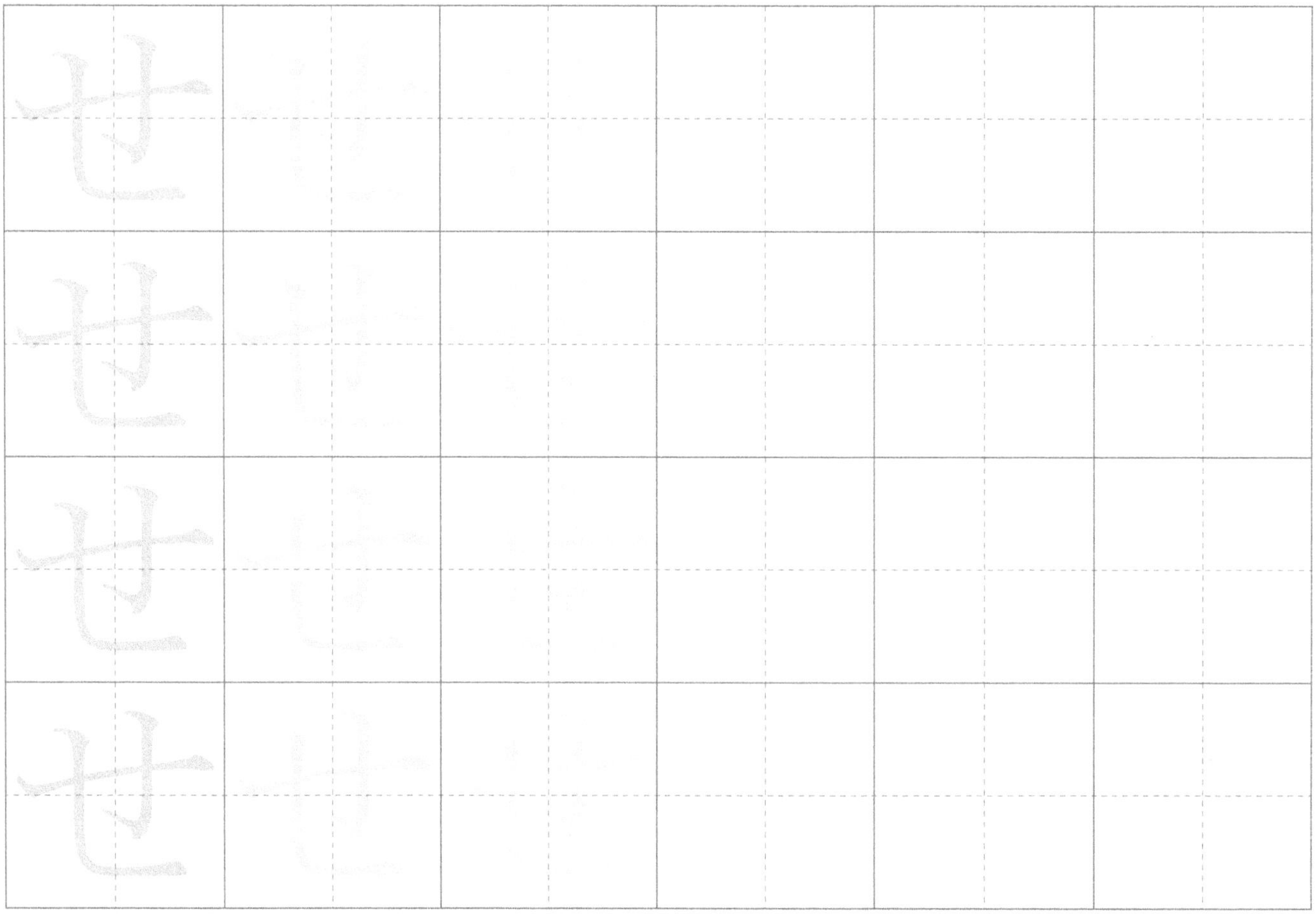

PRACTICE Now practice in these sets of smaller cells

そ そ **so**

SPEAK   Pronounced like the 'so' in soy.

LEARN   This kana is created with a single zig-zag stroke; stop.

Start by making the 'Z' shape in the top half, before adding the 'C' shape below - don't lift your pen from the page. The 'C' shape should end without any upwards motion. Make sure that your middle horizontal line is longer than the top one. Whilst rare, you may see this character displayed as two strokes in some fonts.

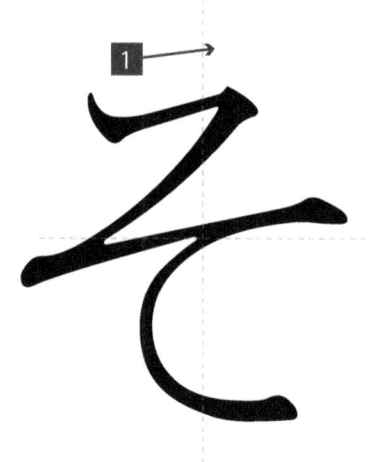

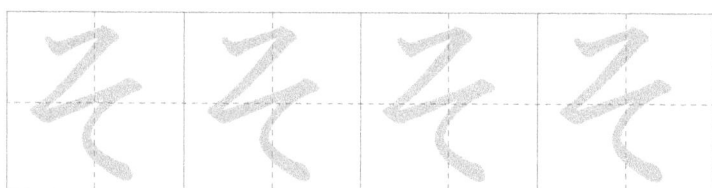

WRITE   First, draw this character in the large cells below

PRACTICE   Now practice in these sets of smaller cells

43

た た **ta**

SPEAK — Pronounced like the 'ta' in target.

LEARN — This kana is drawn with four strokes; they are all stops.

Make a lower case 't' shape, with the vertical line pointing down and left. Make this in the left half of the cell, so there is room for the next part. Your third stroke creates a small curved mark to the right of the T shape and stroke four is made below, with an opposite curve to the previous stroke. The final two strokes should look like they are almost connecting to make a circular shape.

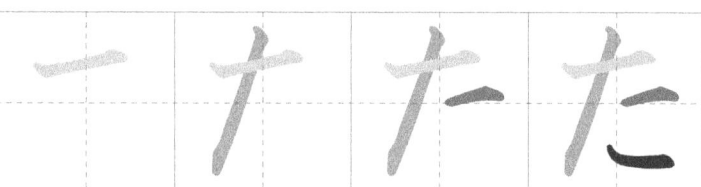

WRITE

First, draw this character in the large cells below

PRACTICE   Now practice in these sets of smaller cells

ち ち chi

SPEAK — Pronounced just like the 'chi' in tai-chi.

LEARN — This kana is drawn with two strokes; stop, fade.

We write this character as a mirror image of さ, but there is no need to lift your pen. Draw your first mark from left to right, at a slight angle. Your second stroke is a slightly diagonal line down and to the left, intersecting with the first. As you approach the bottom, it curves back up and around to the right, making a circular shape and ending with a flick from the page.

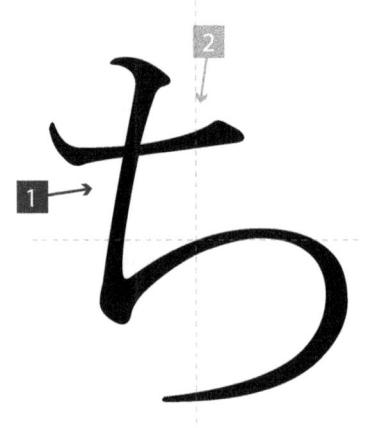

WRITE — First, draw this character in the large cells below

PRACTICE Now practice in these sets of smaller cells

つ つ **tsu**

SPEAK — Pronounced just as the 'tsu' in tsunami, with a silent 't'.

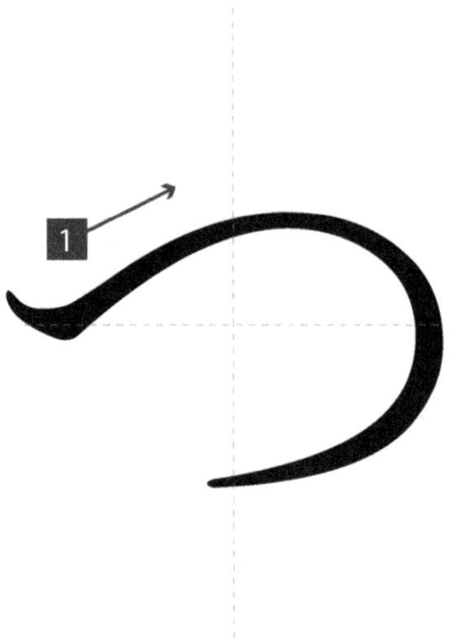

LEARN — This kana is drawn with just a single stroke; fade.

As one of the most simple characters, this kana is made with one long, sweeping curve that fades out at the end. Create the fade by flicking your pen from the page as you approach the end of the arc.

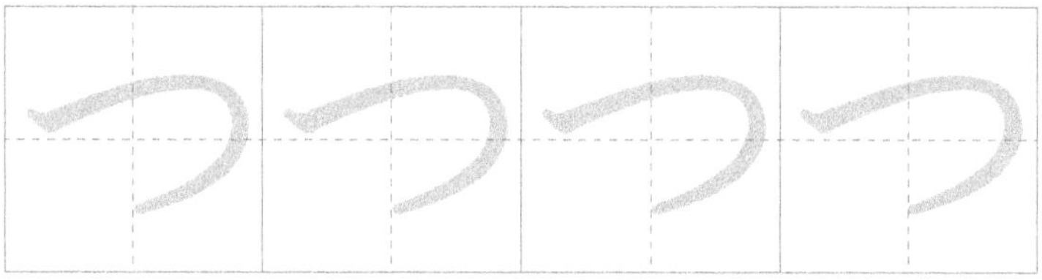

WRITE — First, draw this character in the large cells below

PRACTICE Now practice in these sets of smaller cells

て　て　**te**

SPEAK　Pronounced like the 'te' in ten.

LEARN　This kana is drawn with one stroke; a stop.

In a single stroke, draw your pen from left to right at a slight angle upwards, before moving back along to the left and down. Keep the pen on the paper as you create a large sweeping curve in a 'C' shape. As this is a stop mark, don't flick your pen from the page.

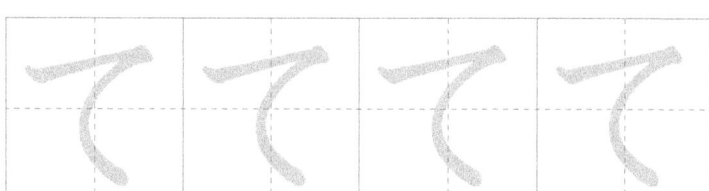

WRITE　First, draw this character in the large cells below

PRACTICE   Now practice in these sets of smaller cells

51

と　と　to

SPEAK　Pronounced like the 'to' in tick-tock.

LEARN　This kana is created with two strokes; stop, stop.

The first mark is a small, slightly slanted line, drawn to the middle of the cell. Your second stroke is a large curved line that meets the end of the first one in the middle. It then bends out left and around towards the bottom right of the cell. The start and end points of your second stroke should be aligned vertically. Your second stroke should not cross the first, but pass through the end.

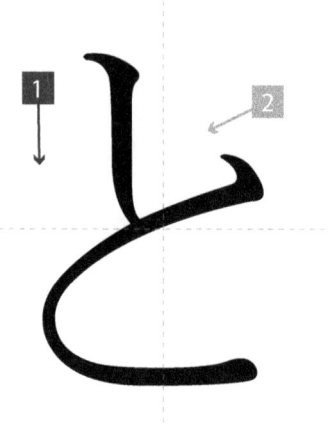

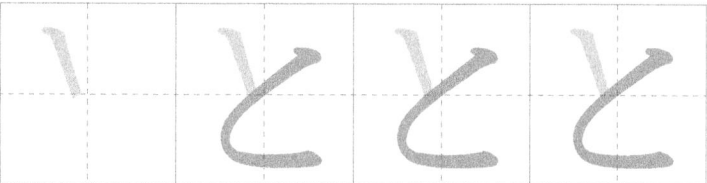

WRITE　　　　　　　　　　　　　　First, draw this character in the large cells below

PRACTICE Now practice in these sets of smaller cells

な　な **na**

SPEAK Pronounced like the 'na' in narwhal.

LEARN This kana has four strokes; stop, stop, jump fade, and stop.

Begin with a short, angled horizontal line on the left. Your second mark is a longer diagonal stroke cutting through the first, down and left - don't make it too long. The third stroke is made as a curved line on the right side, ending with a hane. Just as you lift your pen, immediately start the fourth stroke downwards before looping over itself. End this loop with a stop below the third stroke.

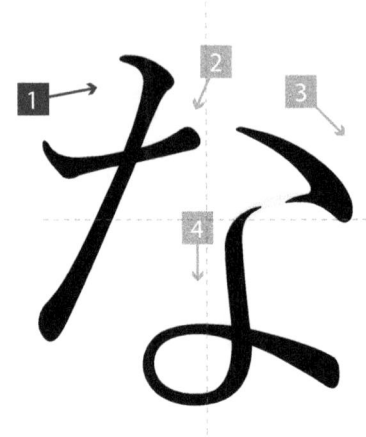

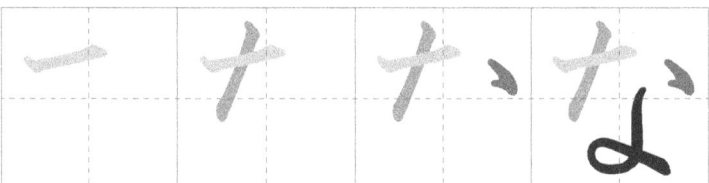

WRITE

First, draw this character in the large cells below

PRACTICE

Now practice in these sets of smaller cells

に に ni

SPEAK — Pronounced like the 'nee' in needle, but shorter.

LEARN — This kana has three strokes; a jump fade, and two stops.

Much like previous characters, begin with a vertical line down on the left side, and end with a hane upwards to the right. Your second mark is almost a continuation from the hane, and is a small curved horizontal line. The last mark is made as a curve in the opposite direction, almost making a circle. Don't flick your pen off the end here, as it is a stop mark.

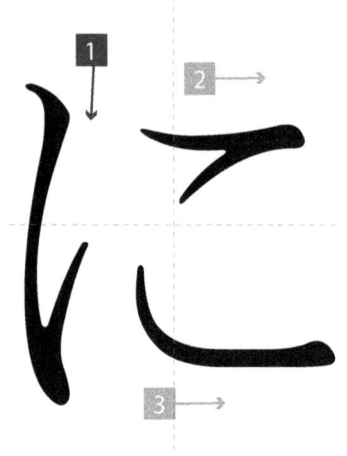

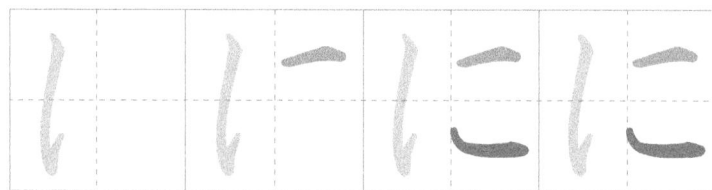

WRITE — First, draw this character in the large cells below

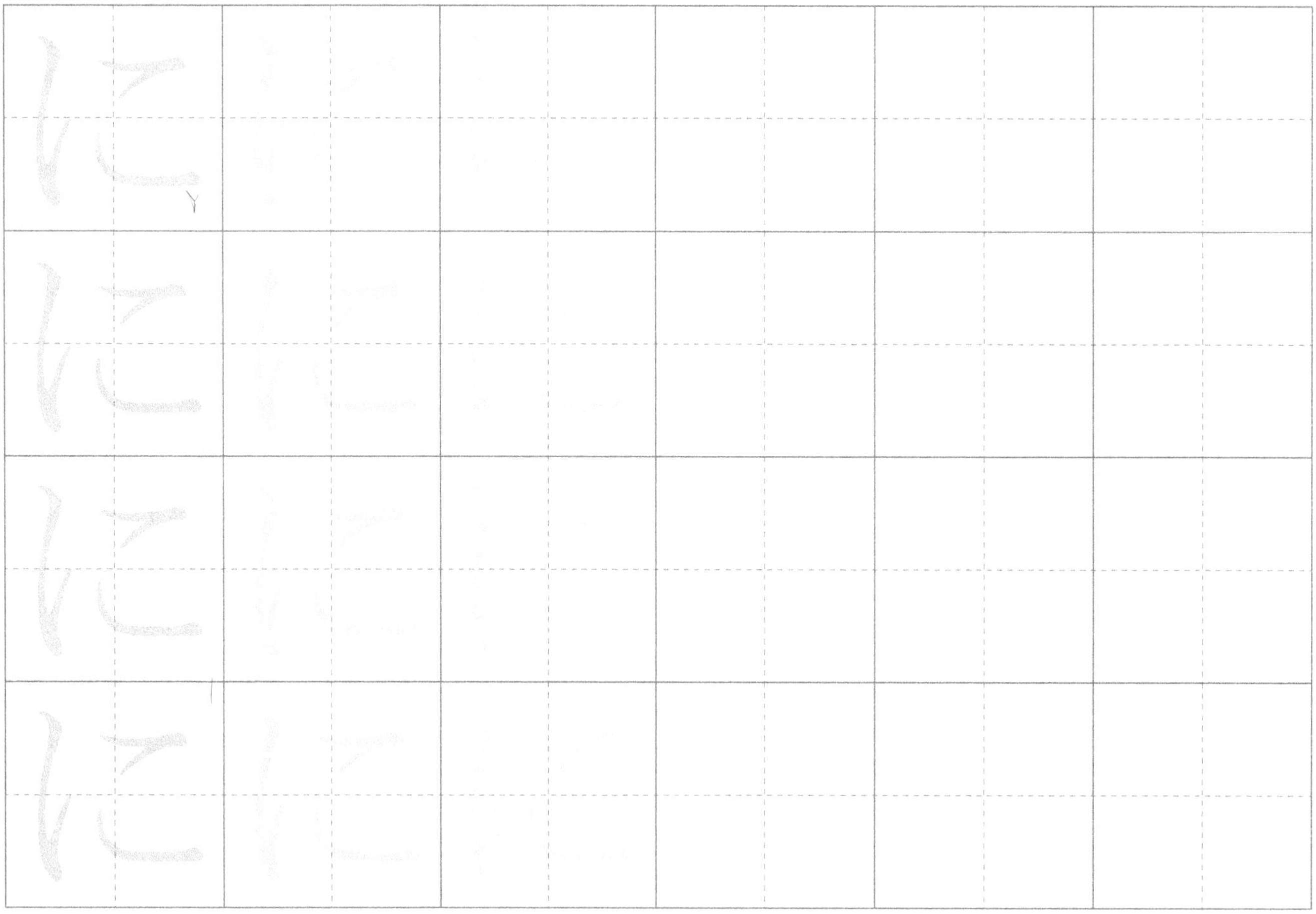

PRACTICE   Now practice in these sets of smaller cells

ぬ ぬ **nu**

SPEAK — Pronounced like the 'noo' in noodles but short.

LEARN — Drawn with two strokes; a stop and a long looping stop.

Start by drawing a slightly curved line at an angle. Your second mark begins at a similar sort of height, but curves back towards the first. It then loops up and back over to the right. As your pen approaches the lower right of the cell, loop back over and to the right. Take care to match the spaces between the lines in the example so that your character is well-balanced.

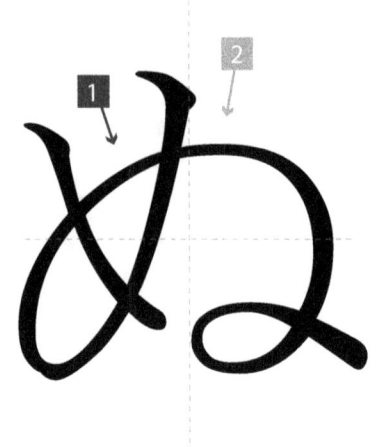

WRITE

First, draw this character in the large cells below

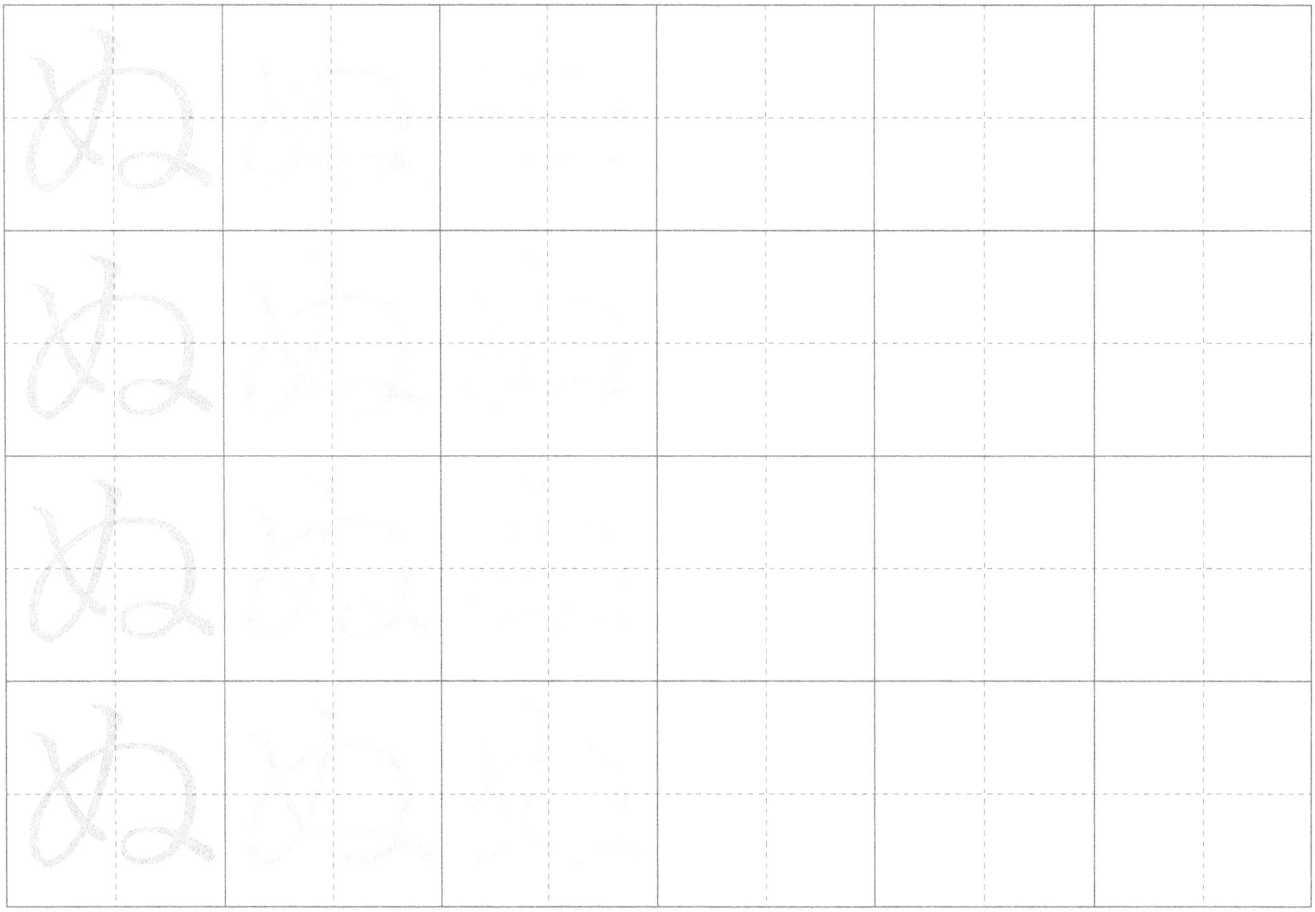

PRACTICE Now practice in these sets of smaller cells

ね ね **ne**

SPEAK — Pronounced like the 'ne' in nest.

LEARN — This kana is drawn with two strokes; stop, long stop.

Draw the vertical line from top to bottom. Start your second stroke with a short horizontal line that passes over the first, before moving your pen down to the left side. Without taking your pen from the page, the second stroke returns upward and continues to create a large arc. As you approach the bottom right, make a small loop back over to the right to complete the character.

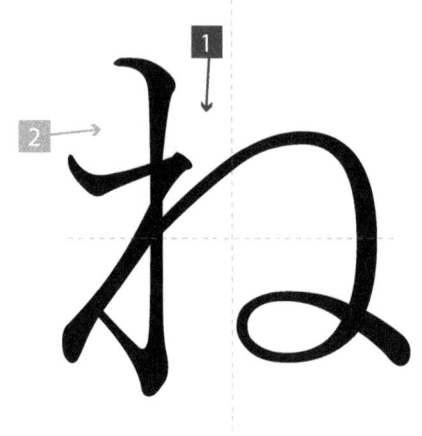

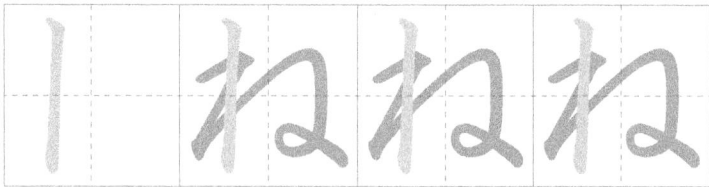

WRITE

First, draw this character in the large cells below

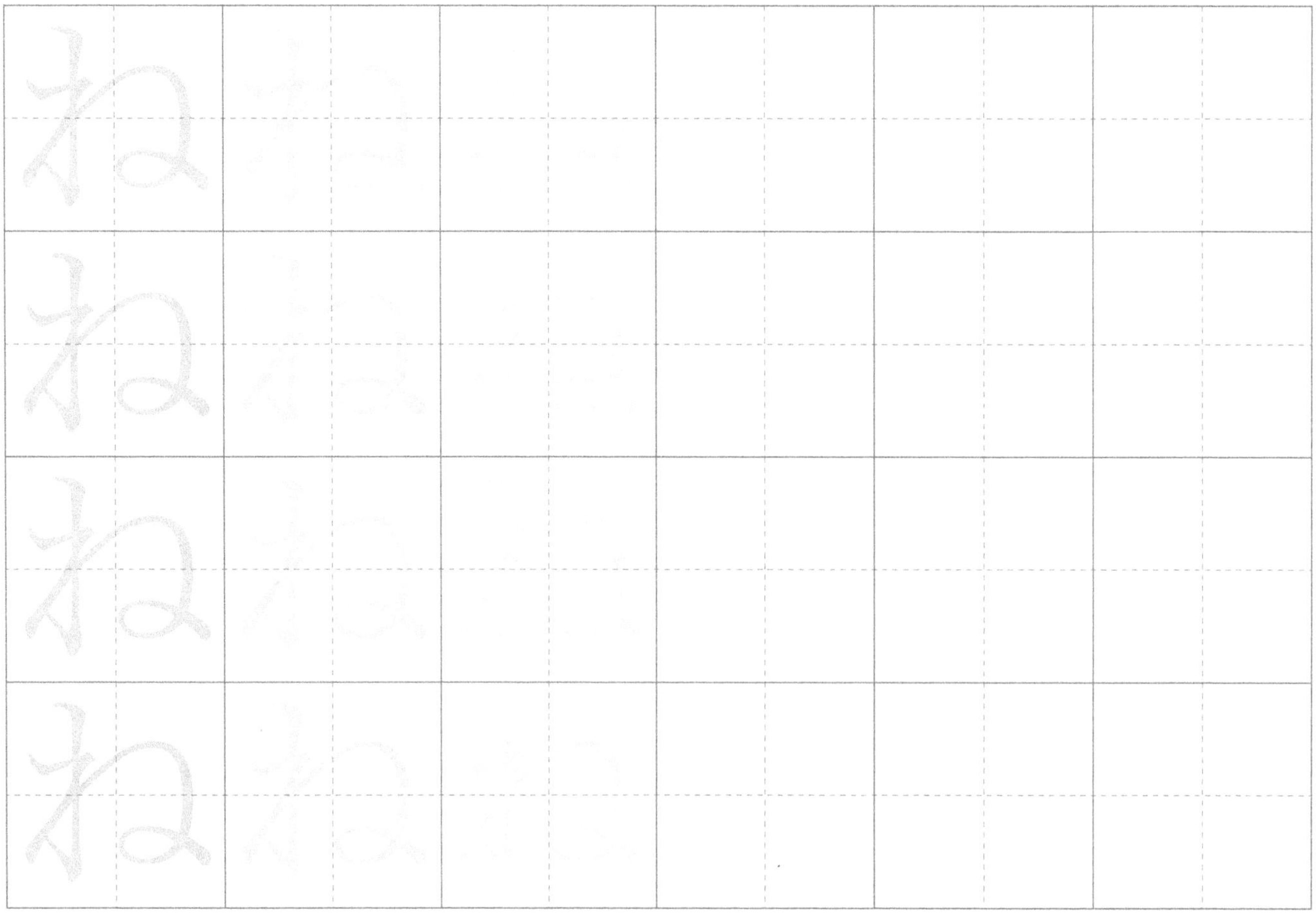

PRACTICE Now practice in these sets of smaller cells

の の **no**

SPEAK Pronounced like the 'no' in nose.

LEARN This kana is written with one stroke; a long fade.

Starting from the upper center part of the cell, draw your pen down and diagonally to the left. From the bottom of this line, move your pen up and over to the right in a large circular motion, passing through the point you started from. When passing across your start point, be sure not to draw your curve too low and allow the vertical line to protrude above. Bring the arc around and flick your pen.

WRITE First, draw this character in the large cells below

PRACTICE   Now practice in these sets of smaller cells

は は ha

SPEAK — Pronounced as the 'ha' when laughing, like ha-ha.

LEARN — Draw this kana with three strokes; jump, stop, loop stop.

Your first two strokes will be similar to hiragana け, with a curved vertical stroke ending in a hane. The second stroke is a shorter horizontal line to the right. Your third stroke will pass through the second, drawn vertically downwards and ending with a small loop over itself to the right.

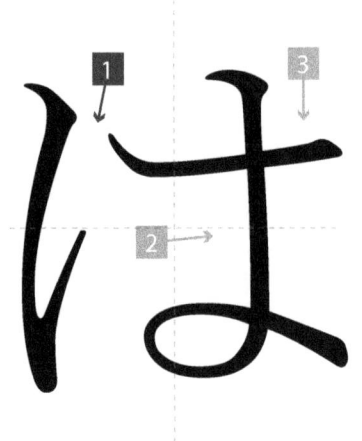

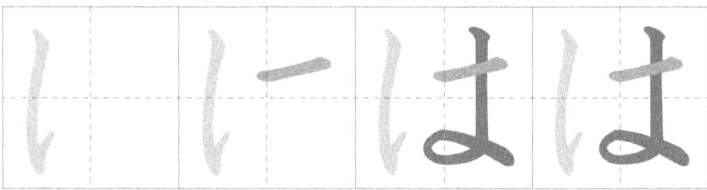

WRITE

First, draw this character in the large cells below

PRACTICE   Now practice in these sets of smaller cells

ひ ひ **hi**

SPEAK — Pronounced like the 'he' in He or She.

LEARN — This kana is drawn with one stroke; a sweeping stop.

Start by making a short, slightly angled line up before returning back a little to the left. Keep your pen on the page as you create a large sweeping curve in a 'U' shape around the lower half of the cell. Once back near the top, and without lifting your pen, trace back a little and then away to the right with a curved line to a stop. Don't flick your pen from the paper here.

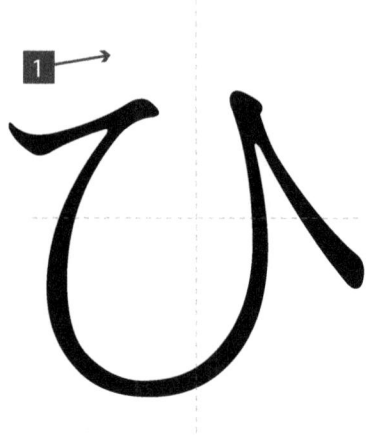

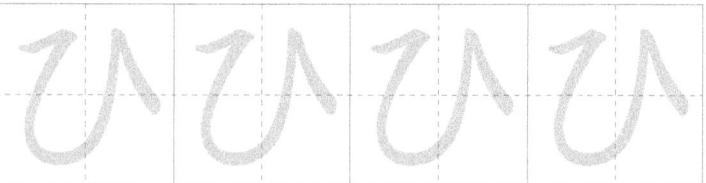

WRITE — First, draw this character in the large cells below

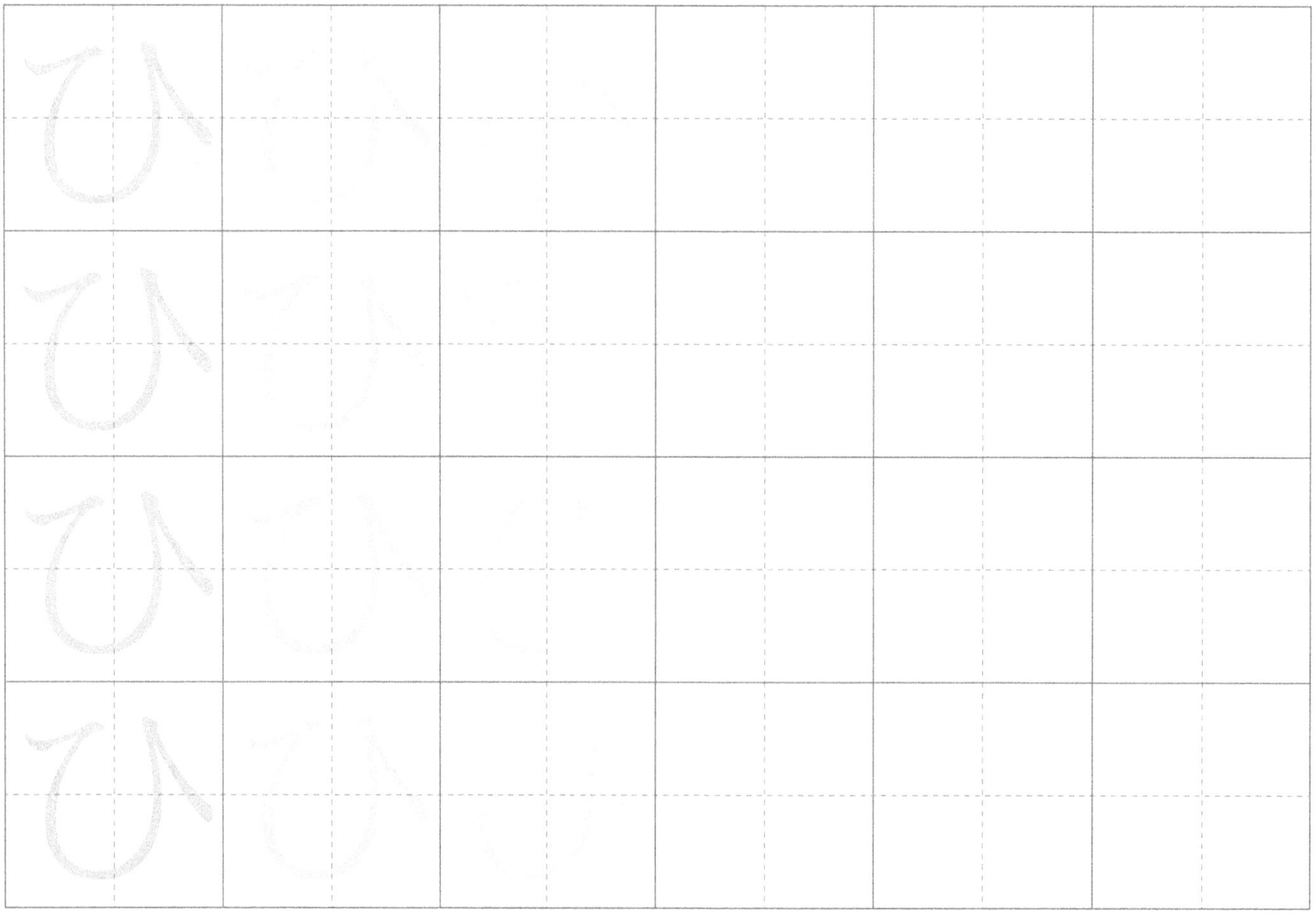

PRACTICE   Now practice in these sets of smaller cells

ふ ふ **fu**

SPEAK — Pronounced as 'hu' like the word 'who'.

LEARN — Drawn with four strokes; jump fade, jump, stop, and stop.

Begin with a short slanted stroke that ends with a hane at the top in the center. Your second stroke is then a sort of nose shape that should be ended with a flick towards the start of stroke three. This is another short slanted line ending with a hane, up and to the right. For the fourth, lift your pen to the right side where you draw the final, short curved line.

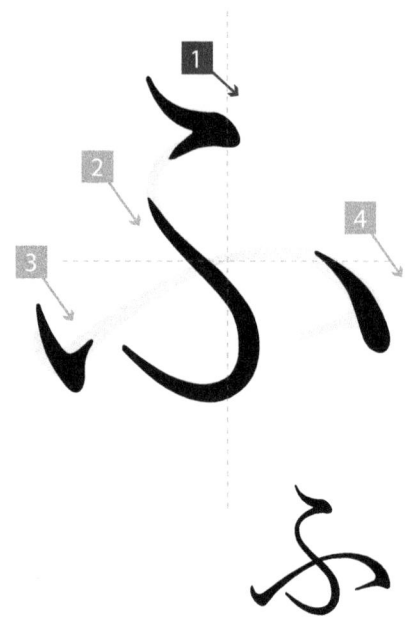

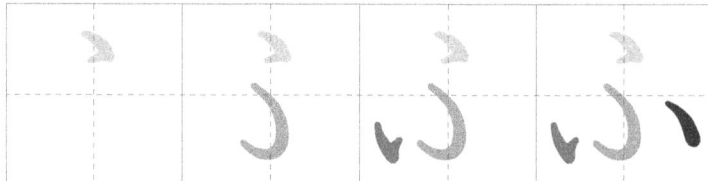

WRITE

First, draw this character in the large cells below

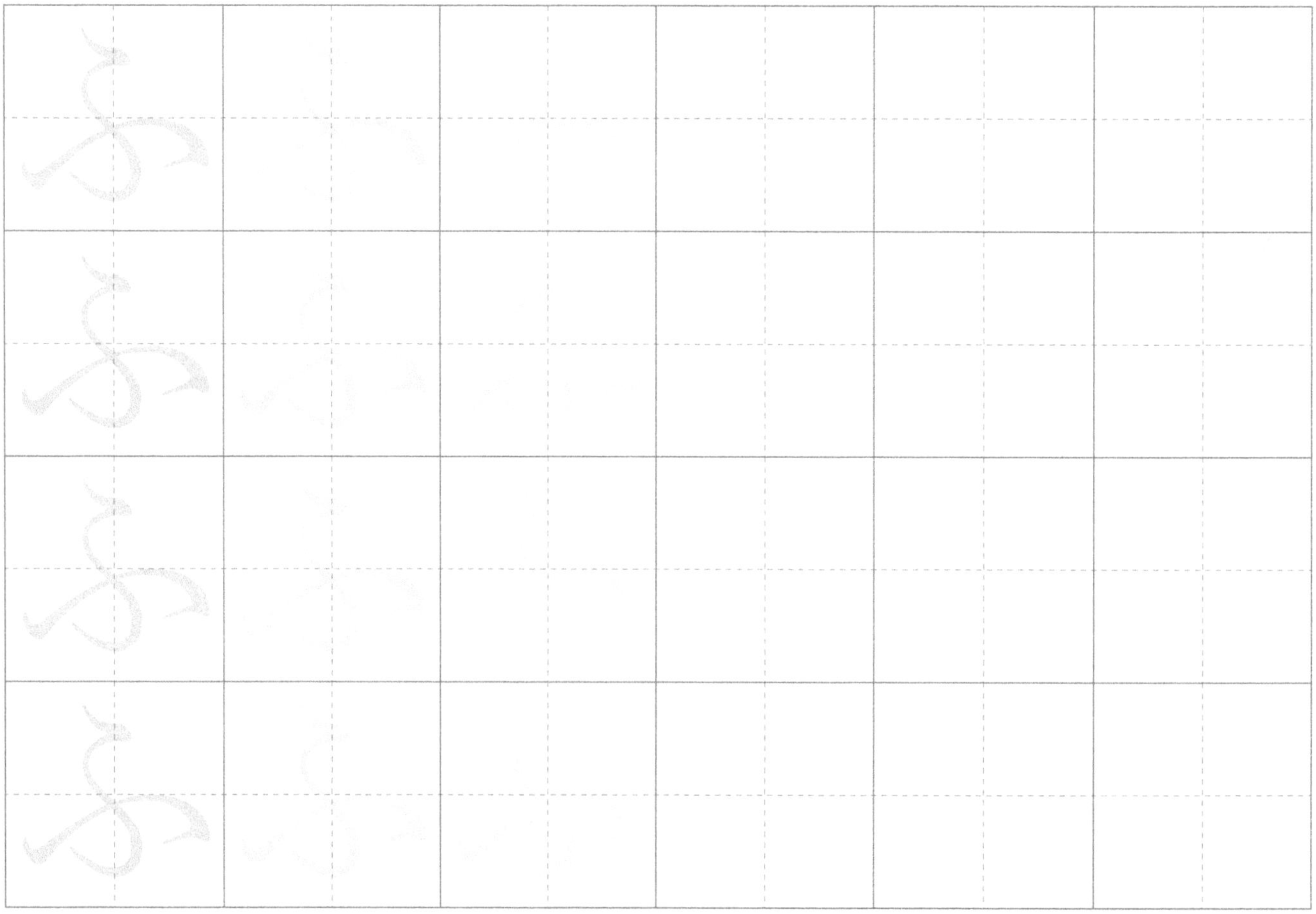

PRACTICE Now practice in these sets of smaller cells

へ ～ **he**

SPEAK — Pronounced like the 'he' in Helen.

LEARN — This kana is made with one stroke; a stop.

Start in the middle on the left of the cell and draw your pen diagonally up and right a short way - but don't pass across the center guideline. Without lifting your pen, continue to draw the longer diagonal line down and to the right. The 'top' of this inverted 'V' shape should not be in the center.

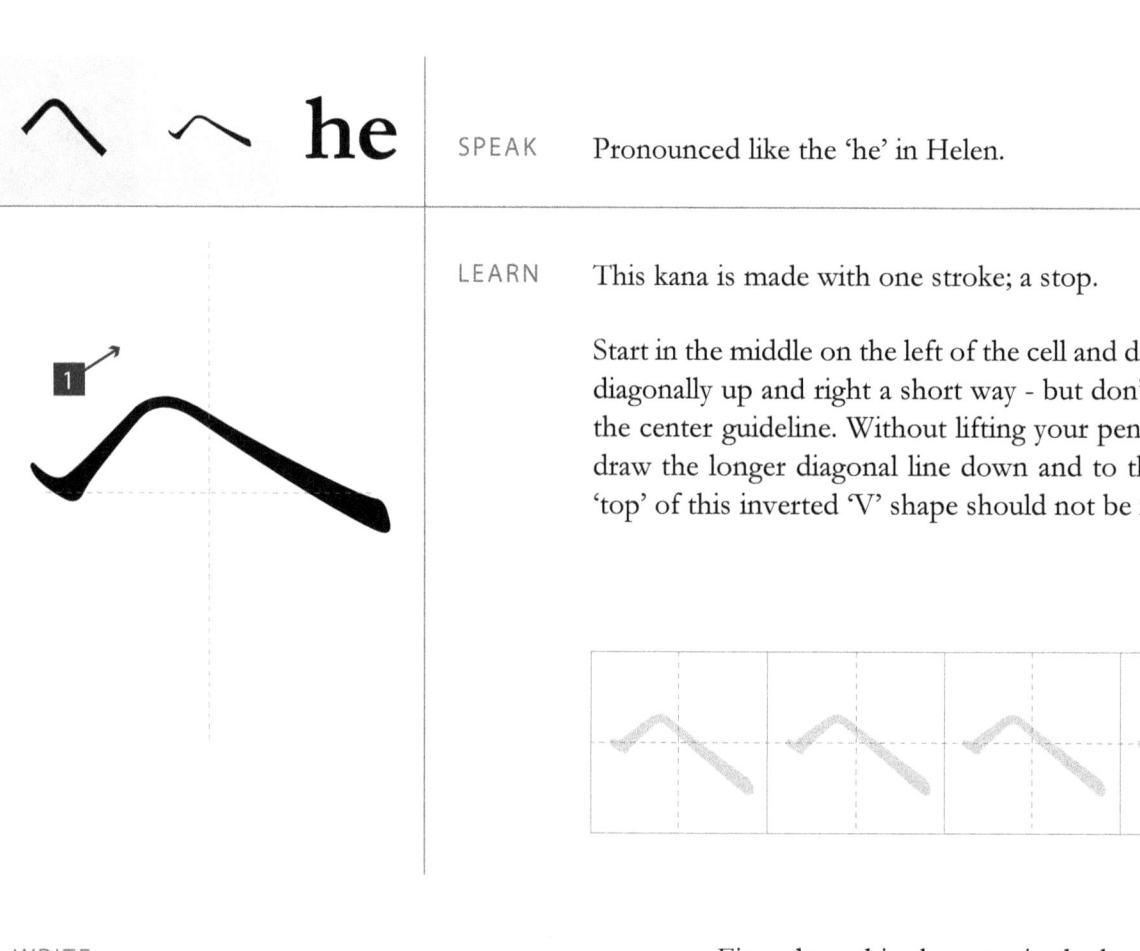

WRITE — First, draw this character in the large cells below

PRACTICE   Now practice in these sets of smaller cells

ほ ほ ho

SPEAK — Pronounced like the 'ho' in home.

LEARN — This has four strokes; jump fade, stop, stop, loop stop.

Just as with the first strokes of は, に, and け, start with a curved vertical line that ends with a hane. Both the second and third strokes are short parallel lines in the upper right. Your final mark should start on the second line - be careful not to begin above it. Move your pen down, through the third stroke, and end with a loop back over your line to the right.

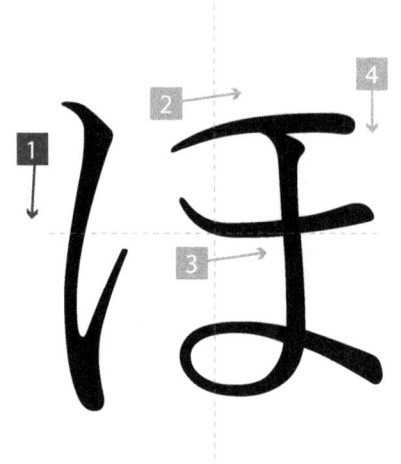

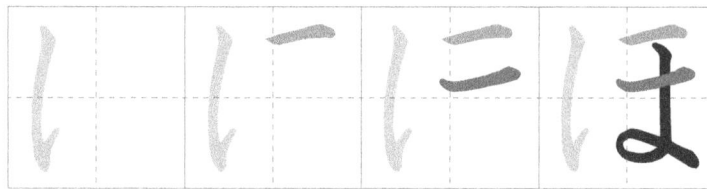

WRITE — First, draw this character in the large cells below

PRACTICE Now practice in these sets of smaller cells

ま ま **ma**

SPEAK   Pronounced like the 'ma' in market.

LEARN   Drawn with three strokes; stop, stop, looping stop.

Begin drawing this kana with parallel horizontal lines, both drawn from left to right. The first one should be a little longer than the second. Your third mark starts from the top, cuts through the first two strokes, and ends with a loop at the bottom. The key to accurately drawing this kana lies in not making the first strokes too long, yet still a little wider than the loop at the end.

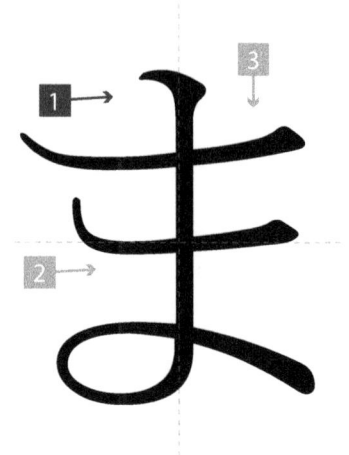

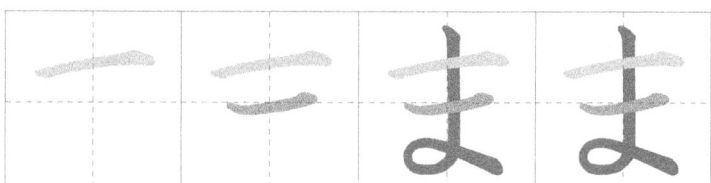

WRITE   First, draw this character in the large cells below

PRACTICE   Now practice in these sets of smaller cells

み み mi

SPEAK — Pronounced just like 'me'.

LEARN — Drawn with two strokes; long looping stop, and a fade.

Start your first stroke with a short horizontal line, then move your pen down and to the left. Without taking your pen from the page, make a loop at the bottom and finish the stroke with off with an arc to the right. Your second stroke is a curve, moving down and left, and cutting through the arc from the first stroke. Flick your pen from the page to fade this stroke out at the end.

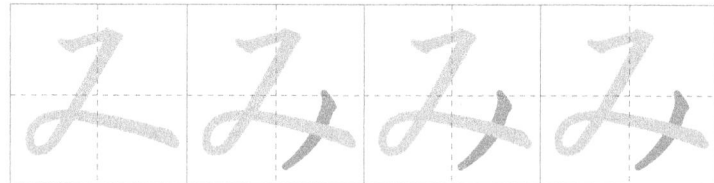

WRITE — First, draw this character in the large cells below

PRACTICE

Now practice in these sets of smaller cells

む　む **mu**

SPEAK　Pronounced like 'moo' but in move.

LEARN　Draw this kana with three strokes; stop, looping fade, stop.

We start drawing this kana in a similar way to す, with a horizontal line on the left side of the cell. The second mark begins at the top and is drawn down, through the first stroke, and then forms a loop below the center. Keeping your pen on the paper after the loop, draw down, across to the right, and then sharply up. Stop before going as high as the first stroke. Finish with a short slanted line.

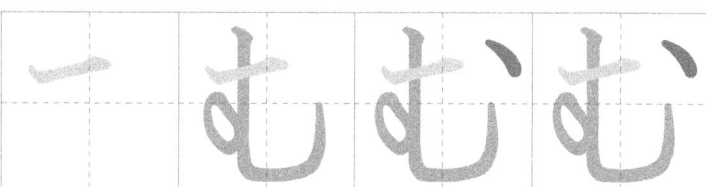

WRITE　　　　　　　　　　　　　First, draw this character in the large cells below

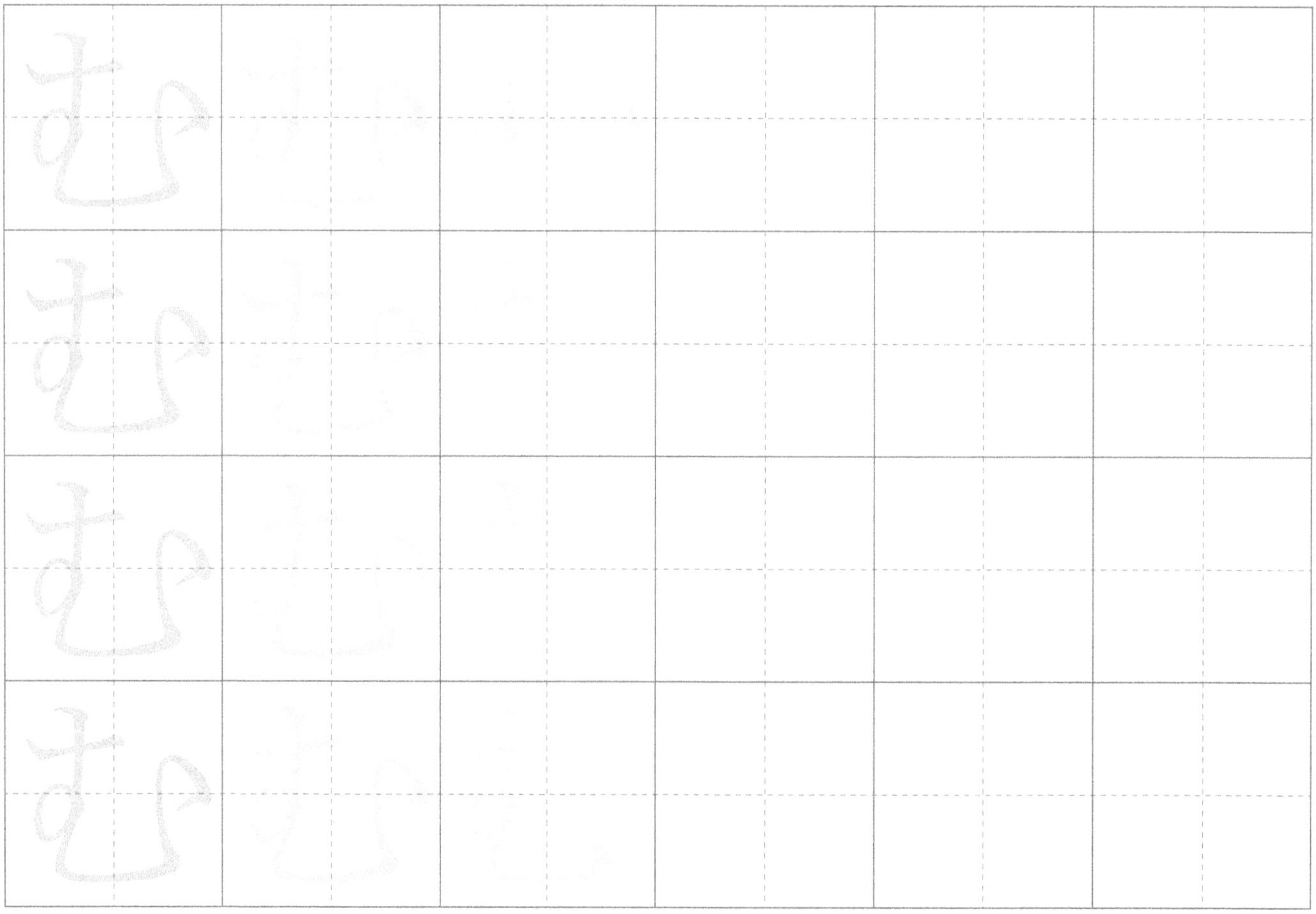

PRACTICE   Now practice in these sets of smaller cells

 **me**

SPEAK — Pronounced as 'meh' like the 'me' in mend.

LEARN — This kana is drawn with two strokes; stop, long fade.

We write this in a similar way to ぬ, except without a loop at the end. First, draw the curved diagonal line down and to the right. The second stroke begins at a similar height to the first, but curves the opposite way. Continue this stroke around in a large circular motion but flick your pen from the paper at the end. Try to match the spaces between lines to create an accurate character.

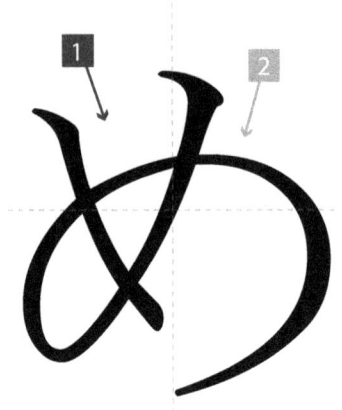

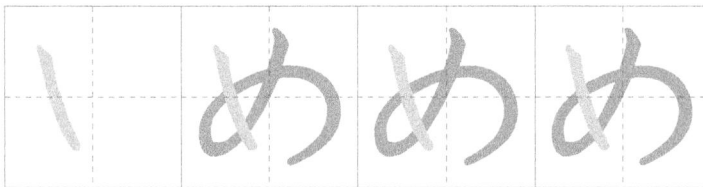

WRITE — First, draw this character in the large cells below

PRACTICE   Now practice in these sets of smaller cells

も も **mo**

SPEAK — Pronounced just like the 'mo' in more.

LEARN — This kana has three strokes; long fade, stop, stop.

Just like hiragana し, we start by drawing the shape of a fishing hook and ending with a flick of the pen as it curves around. Your second and third strokes are two parallel, horizontal lines that cut across the first stroke. This can also be seen with the second and third strokes connected in some fonts, shown in the smaller image on the left.

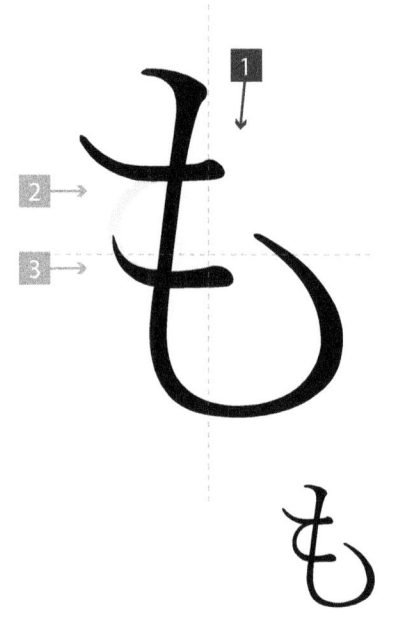

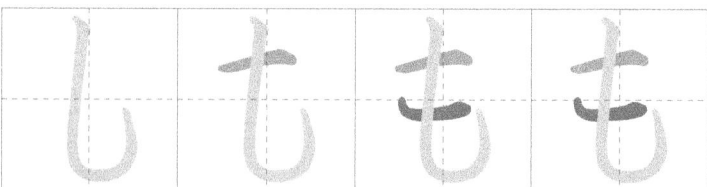

WRITE — First, draw this character in the large cells below

PRACTICE Now practice in these sets of smaller cells

や や **ya**

SPEAK Pronounced like the 'ya' in yard'

LEARN Draw this kana with three strokes; fade, jump, stop.

Your first stroke starts as a shallow diagonal line up and to the right, before curving back around. The second stroke is a short line at the top near the center. The third and final mark is a longer diagonal line from upper left to lower right - it should intersect with the first stroke about a third of the way across from the left. Also seen with strokes 2 and 3 connected, shown in the smaller image to the left.

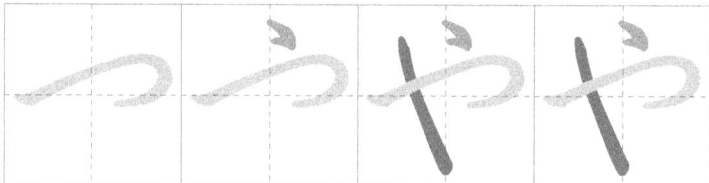

WRITE   First, draw this character in the large cells below

PRACTICE   Now practice in these sets of smaller cells

SPEAK · Pronounced like the 'u' in universal.

LEARN · This kana is drawn with two strokes; fade, fade.

Begin with a slightly curved line downwards before moving back up a little. Without taking your pen from the page, continue by drawing a large curve that almost closes as a circle on itself. Your second stroke is a vertical line that curves down to the left, cutting through the large curve of the first. Finish the stroke by flicking your pen from the paper to fade it out.

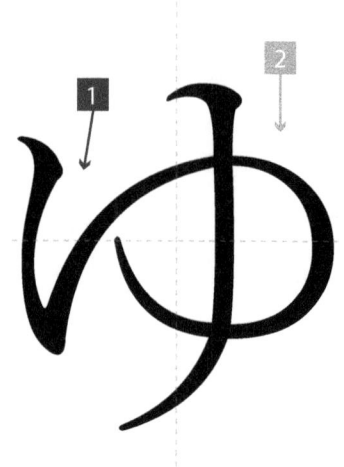

WRITE · First, draw this character in the large cells below

PRACTICE Now practice in these sets of smaller cells

SPEAK   Pronounced just like the 'yo' in yo-yo.

LEARN   This kana is drawn with two strokes; jump fade, stop.

The first mark is a short horizontal line, starting at the center and moving out to the right. Your second stroke begins as a vertical line from the upper center of the cell, and is drawn down towards the bottom before ending with a small loop over itself and stopping in the bottom right. Don't flick the pen here, as this is a stop mark.

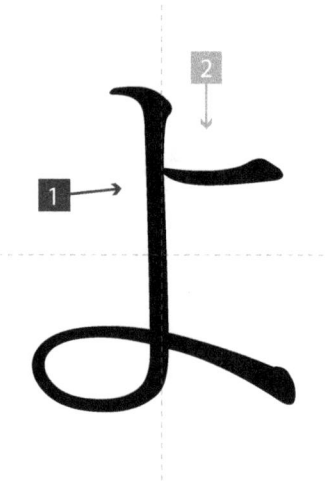

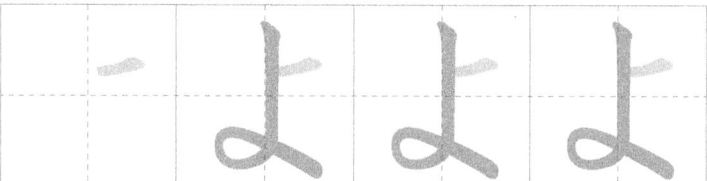

WRITE   First, draw this character in the large cells below

PRACTICE Now practice in these sets of smaller cells

| ら ら | **ra** |

SPEAK Pronounced like the 'ra' in ramen.

LEARN This kana is drawn with two strokes; jump, and a long fade.

The first stroke is a relatively short line, made at an angle near the top of the cell. Then, in a similar way to drawing the number 5, the next mark moves vertically down and then out to the right in a large curve. The curve should move up a little, before turning to come back around and down. End with a flick of your pen. This character can also be seen as a single joined up shape.

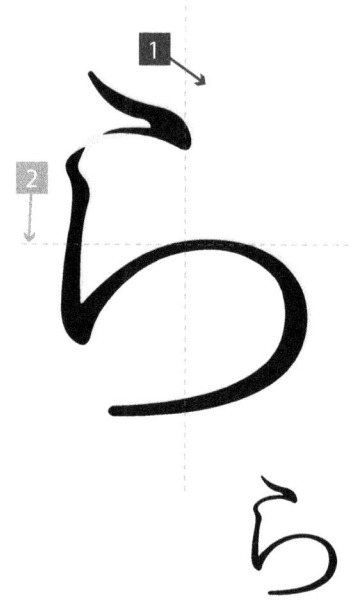

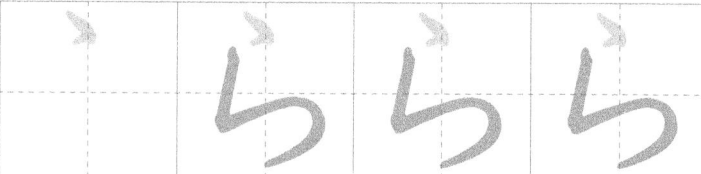

WRITE First, draw this character in the large cells below

PRACTICE   Now practice in these sets of smaller cells

り り ri

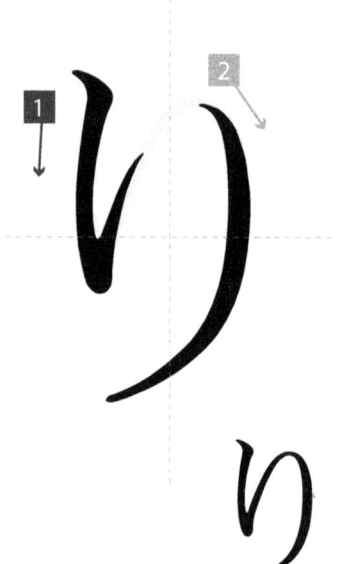

SPEAK   Pronounced like the 'ree' in reef.

LEARN   This kana is drawn with two strokes; jump, fade.

Commonly shown as a single mark, the correct way to write this character is with two strokes. The first is a line going down and finishing with a hane upwards and to the right. As your hane ends, put your pen back down on the paper to create the second stroke. Draw a long curving line down and to the left, flicking your pen from the page at the end to fade it out.

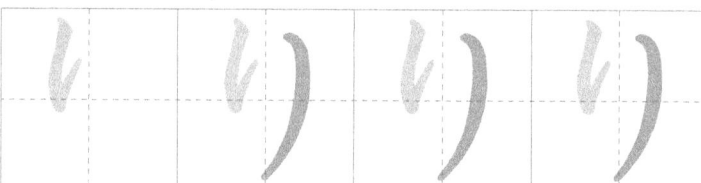

WRITE   First, draw this character in the large cells below

PRACTICE Now practice in these sets of smaller cells

る　る　ru

SPEAK — Pronounced like the 'rew' in brew.

LEARN — This is drawn with one stroke; a long curved zig-zag stop.

This single stroke character begins with a small horizontal line from left to right, before turning and moving down to the left with a longer mark. Without lifting your pen, retrace back up a little and then create a large circular loop, with another, much smaller loop at the end. The smallest loop should not run over or beyond your line, but instead finish on top of it.

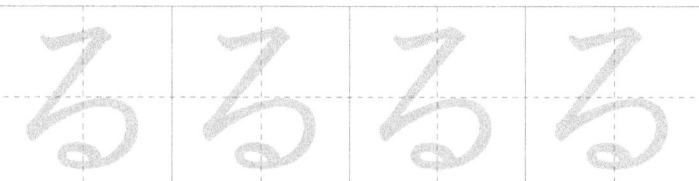

WRITE

First, draw this character in the large cells below

PRACTICE Now practice in these sets of smaller cells

れ　れ　re

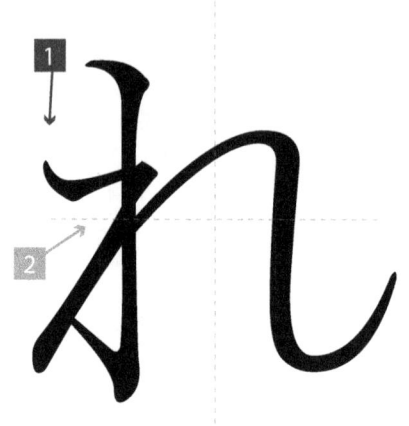

SPEAK — Pronounced like the 're' in rent.

LEARN — Drawn with two strokes; a stop, then a zig-zag fade

Starting with a vertical line from top to bottom, this kana is made with only two strokes. The second begins with a fairly short horizontal line across the first, before going diagonally down and left, crossing the vertical line once more. Without lifting the pen, retrace back upwards then draw a tall wave shape to the right. At the top, drawn down and curve out and up to the right, ending with a flick.

WRITE — First, draw this character in the large cells below

PRACTICE Now practice in these sets of smaller cells

ろ ろ ro

SPEAK Pronounced like the 'ro' in road.

LEARN This kana is drawn with one stroke; zig-zag fade.

We write the ろ in much the same way as writing る, except without a loop at the end. Start with a fairly short horizontal short line from left to right, and follow with a diagonal line down and back to the left. Trace back upwards a little and then finish the stroke off by making the large curve out to the right and back in - all in one smooth action, ending with a flick from the page.

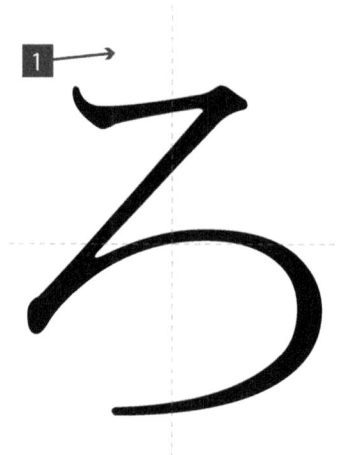

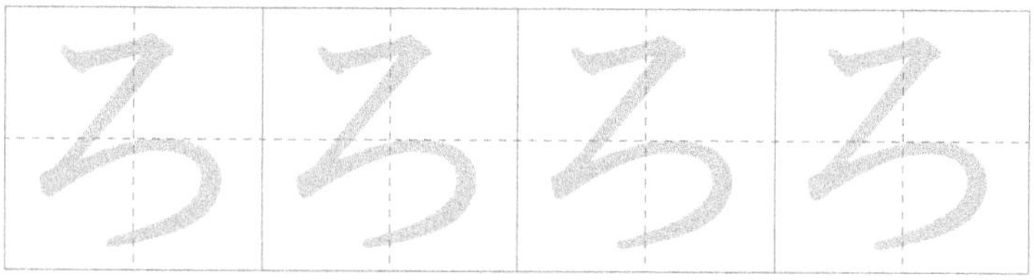

WRITE First, draw this character in the large cells below

PRACTICE Now practice in these sets of smaller cells

わ わ **wa**

SPEAK　Pronounced like the 'wa' in wagon.

LEARN　This kana is drawn with two strokes; stop, zig-zag fade.

Begin with the vertical mark from top to bottom, left of the center and ending with a hane up and left. Your second line passes across the first stroke and then moves diagonally down to the left and cutting through the first one again. Complete this stroke by drawing the large curve out to the right and back around, fading it at the end with a flick.

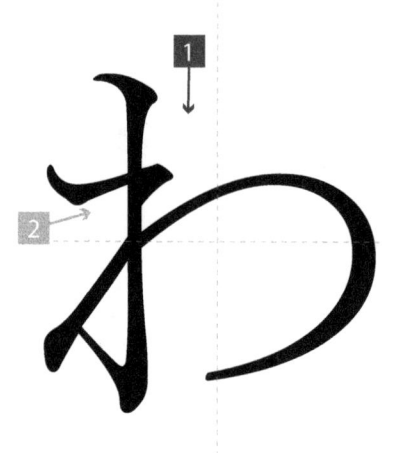

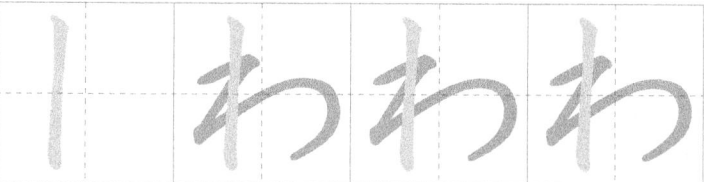

WRITE　　　　　　　　　　　　　　First, draw this character in the large cells below

PRACTICE Now practice in these sets of smaller cells

を を wo*

SPEAK Pronounced like the 'oh' in woah, with a silent 'w'.

LEARN Drawn with three strokes; each of which is a stop.

Your first stroke is a horizontal line from left to right. The second mark begins as a diagonal line crossing the first stroke, before turning up and back down. It should end at a lower point to where your pen turned before. Your third line is a curve that starts from the right side, above the center line, and cuts through the end of the second stroke. It returns to the lower right of the cell, ending with a stop.

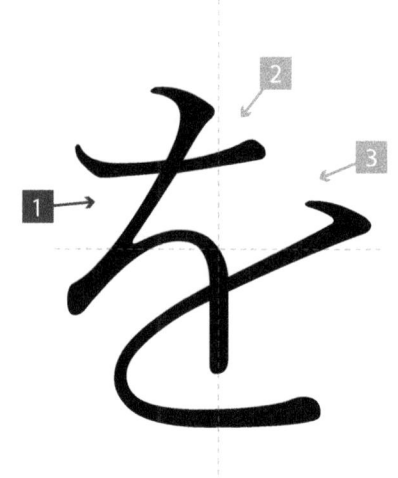

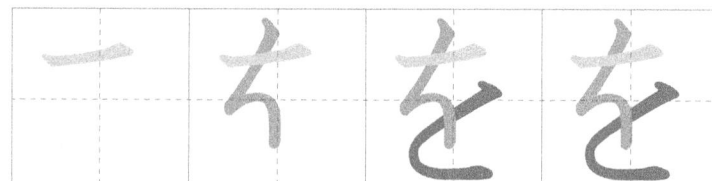

Uncommon kana, used as a particle.

WRITE First, draw this character in the large cells below

PRACTICE   Now practice in these sets of smaller cells

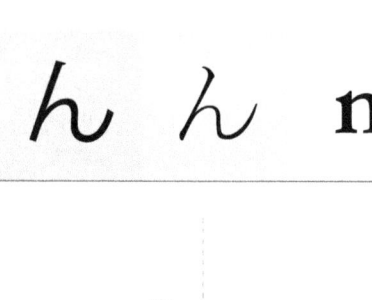

SPEAK	Pronounced like just the 'n' sound in ink.
LEARN	This kana is drawn with one stroke; long fade.
	This character is created with a single stroke. It begins with a diagonal line from the upper center area, down to the lower left. Without lifting your pen, retrace back upwards a little before creating a wave shape - end this stroke and character by flicking your pen from the page to fade the stroke out around the center line area.

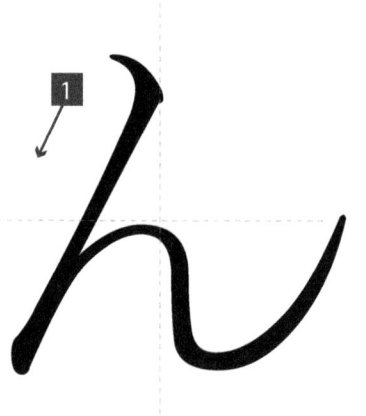

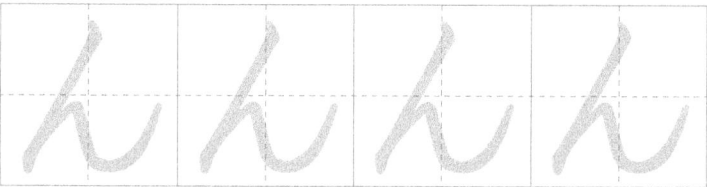

WRITE

First, draw this character in the large cells below

PRACTICE   Now practice in these sets of smaller cells

Part 3

GENKOUYOUSHI
GRID PAPER FOR FURTHER PRACTICE

Part 4

FLASH CARDS
PHOTOCOPY OR CUT OUT & KEEP

a
Pronounced like the 'a' in car or father, but shorter.

i
Pronounced like the 'ee' in eel.

u
Pronounced like the 'oo' in zoo.

e
Pronounced as 'eh' like the 'e' in men.

o
Pronounced like the 'o' in original.

ka
Pronounced like 'car' but without the 'r' sound.

ki
Pronounced like 'key'.

ku
Pronounced like the 'koo' in cuckoo.

ke
Pronounced like the 'ke' in Kenneth.

ko
Pronounced like the 'co' in core.

sa
Pronounced like the 'sa' in sardines.

shi
Pronounced like 'shee' as in sheet.

す	ち	な
せ	し	に
そ	て	ぬ
た	つ	ね

su
Pronounced like the 'su' in super.

chi
Pronounced just like the 'chi' in tai-chi.

na
Pronounced like the 'na' in narwhal.

se
Pronounced like 'say' but with less 'y' sound.

tsu
Pronounced just as the 'tsu' in tsunami, with a silent 't'.

ni
Pronounced like the 'nee' in needle but shorter.

so
Pronounced like the 'so' in soy.

te
Pronounced just like the 'te' in ten.

nu
Pronounced like the 'noo' in noodles but short.

ta
Pronounced like the 'ta' in target.

to
Pronounced like the 'to' in tick-tock.

ne
Pronounced like the 'ne' in nest.

no
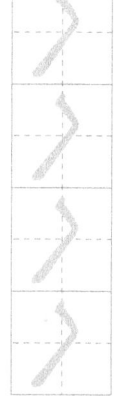
Pronounced like the 'no' in nose.

ha
Pronounced as the 'ha' when laughing, like ha-ha.

hi
Pronounced like the 'he' in He or She.

fu
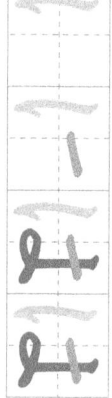
Pronounced as 'hu' like the word 'who'.

he
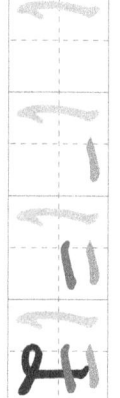
Pronounced like the 'he' in Helen.

ho
Pronounced like the 'ho' in home.

ma
Pronounced like the 'ma' in market.

mi
Pronounced just like 'me'.

mu
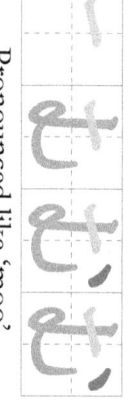
Pronounced like 'moo' but in move.

me
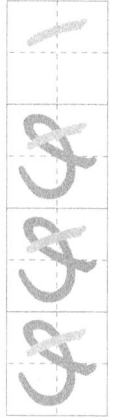
Pronounced like 'meh' like the 'me' in mend.

mo

Pronounced just like the 'mo' in more.

ya
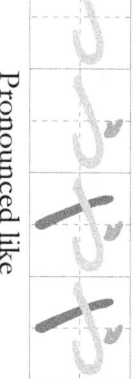
Pronounced like the 'ya' in yard.

む	ち	さ
す	ち	ん
か	ら	
こ	も	

yu
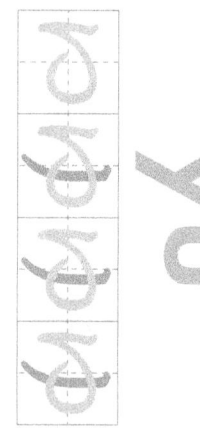
Pronounced like the 'u' in universal.

yo
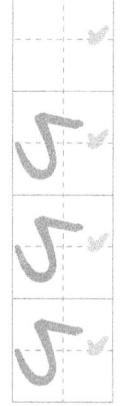
Pronounced just like the 'yo' in yo-yo.

re
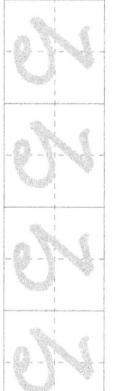
Pronounced like the 're' in rent.

ri
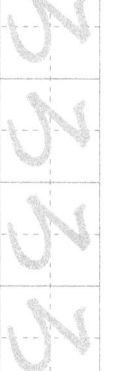
Pronounced like the 'ree' in reef.

ra
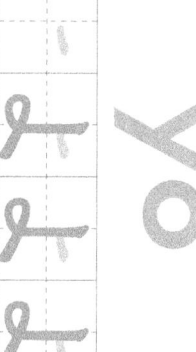
Pronounced like the 'ra' in ramen.

ru
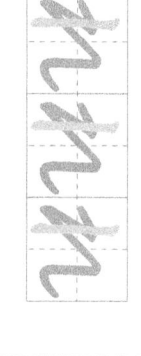
Pronounced like the 'rew' in brew.

ro
Pronounced like the 'ro' in road.

wa
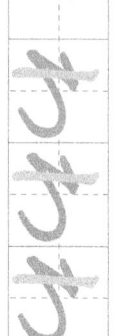
Pronounced like the 'wa' in wagon.

wo
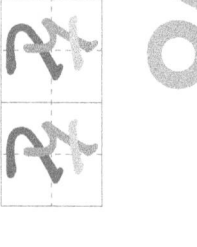
Pronounced like the 'oh' in woah, with a silent 'w'.

n*
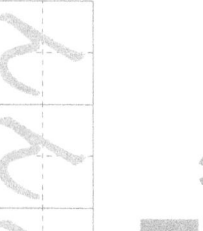
Pronounced like just the 'n' sound in ink.

ありがとう
arigatou

Thank you!

Thank you for choosing our book!

You are now well on your way to learning how to read, write and speak Japanese, and we hope that you enjoyed our Hiragana workbook.

If you enjoyed learning Hiragana with us, we would very much like to hear about your progress in a review!

We are always eager to learn if there is anything we can do to make our books better for future students. We are committed to making the best language learning content available! Please do get in touch with us via email if you had a problem with any of the content in this book:

hello@polyscholar.com

POLYSCHOLAR

www.polyscholar.com

© Copyright 2020 George Tanaka - **All rights reserved.**

Legal Notice: This book is copyright protected. This book is only for personal use. The content contained within this book may not be reproduced, duplicated or transmitted without direct written permission from the author or the publisher. You cannot amend, distribute, sell, use, quote or paraphrase any part of the content within this book, without the consent of the author or publisher.

www.ingramcontent.com/pod-product-compliance
Lightning Source LLC
Chambersburg PA
CBHW060416010526
44107CB00006B/708